IMAGES of America
WHITEFISH BAY

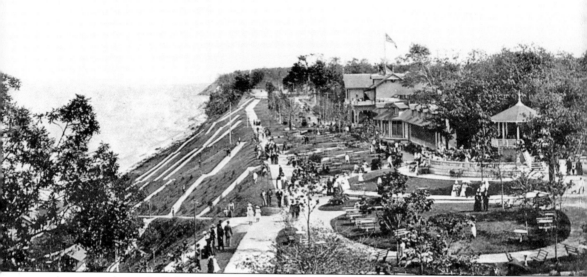

A summer day at the Pabst Whitefish Bay Resort, likely photographed from the top of the Ferris wheel, is captured here. Many paths crisscrossed the lake bluff, permitting ample opportunity for those sporting their Sunday finest to promenade and enjoy the grounds and scenery. (Courtesy of the Whitefish Bay Historical Society.)

ON THE COVER: Employees of the Whitefish Bay Fire Department stand proudly with their equipment in this 1941 photograph. Shown are Engine No. 1, Truck No. 1, and the fire chief's command car, all clean and polished, outside of the village's first firehouse. The firehouse was behind Village Hall at 801 East Lexington Boulevard—approximately the same location as the current North Shore fire department building. Pictured, left to right, are Chief Henry Asen (who served in this capacity between 1928 and 1951), George Kranich, Erwin Hess, Art Heise, Fred Baumeier, Joseph Kassel, William Hoppenrath, and Eugene Wheeler. (Courtesy of the Whitefish Bay Historical Society.)

IMAGES *of America*
WHITEFISH BAY

Thomas H. Fehring

Copyright © 2010 by Thomas H. Fehring
ISBN 978-0-7385-8395-2

Published by Arcadia Publishing
Charleston, South Carolina

Printed in the United States of America

Library of Congress Control Number: 2010928670

For all general information, please contact Arcadia Publishing:
Telephone 843-853-2070
Fax 843-853-0044
E-mail sales@arcadiapublishing.com
For customer service and orders:
Toll-Free 1-888-313-2665

Visit us on the Internet at www.arcadiapublishing.com

CONTENTS

Acknowledgments		6
Introduction		7
1.	Early History of the Area	9
2.	Transportation and Resorts	19
3.	Formation of the Village	35
4.	The Residential Housing Movement	47
5.	Village of Fine Homes	57
6.	Whitefish Bay Commercial Districts	71
7.	Social Infrastructure	87
8.	The Changing Landscape	103
9.	The People of the Village	111

Acknowledgments

I would like to acknowledge and thank the following for their helpful assistance:

Whitefish Bay Historical Society, and especially Carol Krigbaum and her husband, Elkin Gonzalez, for providing numerous historic photographs of the village; the reference librarians at the Whitefish Bay library, for their frequent and helpful assistance; the support of the members of the Whitefish Bay Historic Preservation Commission; the helpful staffs of the Humanities Room at the Milwaukee Public Library and of the Research Room of the Milwaukee Country Historical Society; the assistance of John Pandl, Jim Sponholz, Bill Kregel, Paul Doty, Bill Crowley, Lynn Ehlenbeck, Carolyn Sanger, John Stuhlmacher, Robin Pickering-Iazzi, Jack Prince, Bruce Erickson, Mary Kromarek, O. K. Johnson, and Gail Roeder for contributing photographs for this effort; and my wife, Suzan, for reviewing the text and her understanding of the many hours that I spent working on this project.

Unless otherwise noted, images appear courtesy of the Whitefish Bay Historical Society and the Whitefish Bay Library. They jointly maintain the village's historical collection, which includes the Mimi Bird Files—an invaluable source of village history. Most images were scanned from the historical collection, or obtained directly from the WFB Historical Society's files.

This work could not have been prepared without the previous extensive research of members of the WFB Historical Society, past and present, upon which I relied heavily—most notably the work of Mimi Bird, Ralph Knoernschild, and Lewis Herzog, to whom the village is indebted.

While I have attempted to be thorough in my research, and have relied upon the former distinguished work of village historians, my personal history in Whitefish Bay only extends back to 1973. It is inevitable that errors may have occurred. Most of the history contained in these pages predates that year by decades. If I have misinterpreted some of the pictures, I apologize.

I enjoyed gathering and reviewing early images of the village. I scanned well over 500 photographs—of which only about half could be included in this book. The most difficult task in publishing this book involved the final image selections. Inevitably, many interesting pictures had to be excluded.

INTRODUCTION

This is a history of Whitefish Bay, Wisconsin, told largely through pictures. If it is true that a picture tells 1,000 words, the 200 or so images in this book should convey the story of the village. The reality, of course, is that each picture provides a different perspective of the fabric that represents the village. Several hundred photographs cannot fully capture the lives of the many thousands of residents that have lived here.

This pictorial journey is divided into chapters that highlight the early history of the area, the impact of transportation, the early resort industry, and the movement to form a village by early settlers interested in providing an education for their children. It then covers the early residential housing movement and illustrates some of the architecturally significant homes that were built during the first part of the last century—leading to the village's Gold Coast distinction.

For residents of the village, however, the most interesting photographs may be those of the early businesses in the Whitefish Bay commercial districts (Silver Spring Drive and Henry Clay Street) and the social infrastructure of the community, including its schools, churches, clubs, and other organizations.

The final chapters are devoted to illustrating some of the changes that have occurred in Whitefish Bay over the years and the lives of the people that have resided in our community.

While there are exceptions, most of the images are from the period of 1880 to about 1940—representing the early history of the village.

It is hoped that readers enjoy this trip through Whitefish Bay's past.

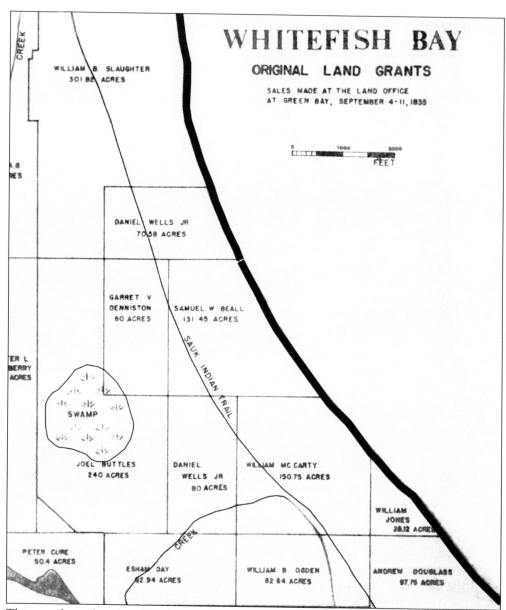

This map shows the original land grants for the area that now encompasses the village of Whitefish Bay. It is based on sales made at the Green Bay land office in 1835. The map also approximates the location of the Sauk Indian Trail and the various wetland areas.

One

Early History of the Area

The area that encompasses the present village of Whitefish Bay was once part of lands occupied by the Menomonee Indian tribe. While little is known of tribal life in the area, the land undoubtedly afforded good hunting and fishing. The tribe also traveled throughout the region, often using the Salk Trail, a footpath that followed the high land between the Milwaukee River and Lake Michigan and extended as far north as Green Bay.

The Menomonees' title to the area was conveyed to the United States by treaty on February 8th, 1831. The land was quickly surveyed and on March 17, 1835, Wisconsin incorporated it as part of the town of Milwaukee. Parcels were sold in auction by the U.S. Government Land Office in Green Bay in September, 1835.

Most of the initial land purchasers quickly divided their properties and sold parcels to settlers who began clearing and farming the land. The Whitefish Bay area was a good place to live. It had fertile land and good drinking water. The adjacent lake and rivers provided an abundance of fish.

Along with the farmers came fishermen to the Bay. In 1862, John Luck, a fisherman from the fishing district near Green Bay, arrived in the area. Luck, with the help of William Consaul one of the first farmers in the area, constructed the first pound net in the bay. The fish that that were caught most often was the whitefish—eventually leading to the village's name.

Many farmhouses of early settlers of the village are still located throughout Whitefish Bay. Two notable examples include William H. and Ruth Consaul's home, located at 716 East Silver Spring Drive and believed to have been built in 1856, and Johann Bauch's farmhouse, which was constructed between 1863 and 1865 and is located at 5007 North Idlewild Avenue.

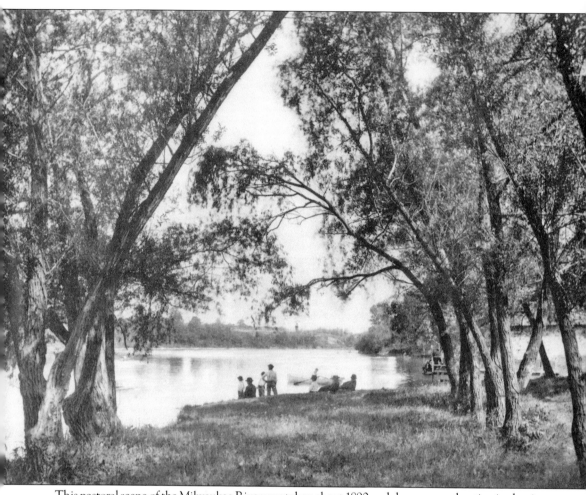
This pastoral scene of the Milwaukee River was taken about 1890 and shows a man boating in the river while a family reclines on the river bank. (Photograph from *Milwaukee: 100 Photogravures*.)

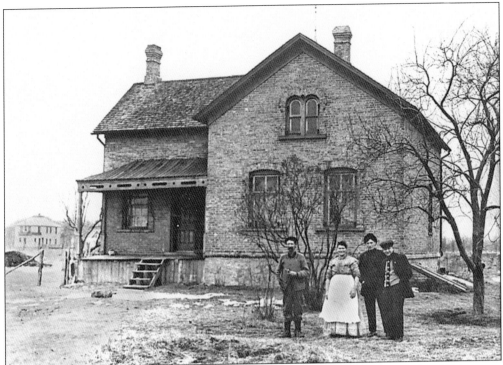

This was Johann Busch's farmhouse, built between 1863 and 1865. It originally faced Fairmount Avenue and had to be moved 48 feet to its present site when Idlewild Avenue was constructed in 1926. Johann Busch originally farmed five acres between Fairmount Avenue and Henry Clay Street. This photograph was taken in 1909 at the original site of the house. Pictured are Frank and Caroline Christi Stahl and their son George. The other individual is unidentified.

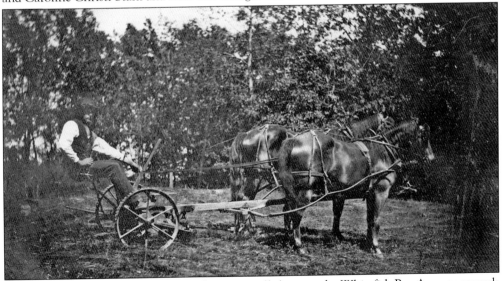

William Staffeld is plowing a field on what eventually became the Whitefish Bay Armory grounds in this scan of an original tintype photograph. It is likely that the photograph was made by Pechtel's Tintype Gallery, which was located in Welcome Park, near the Pabst Whitefish Bay Resort. Judging from the type of tintype, it appears that this photograph dates between 1870 and 1885.

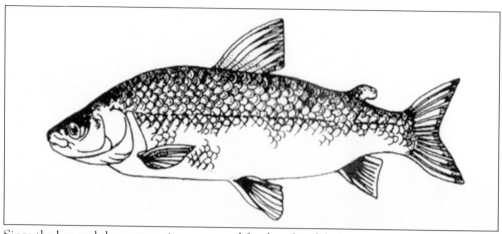

Since the bay and the community, are named for the whitefish, it seems appropriate to include this illustration. This drawing, by Christine Kohler of the University of Wisconsin Sea Grant Institute, appeared in *Fishing the Great Lakes: An Environmental History 1783–1933* by Margaret Beattie Bogue, published by the University of Wisconsin Press in 2000.

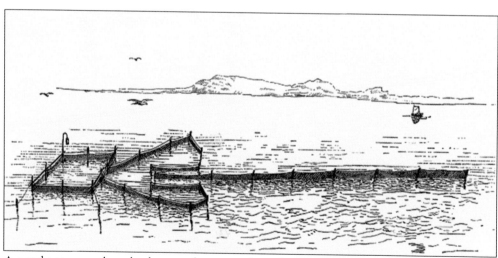

A pond net uses a long leader net, shown on the right two-thirds of this image, to guide fish toward the heart-shaped core, from which they swim through a tunnel into the pot of the net. Once in the pot, fish were effectively trapped and could easily be harvested by the fisherman. L. Kumlien drew this for the *Review of the Fisheries of the Great Lakes in 1885*, a U.S. Commission of Fish and Fisheries report.

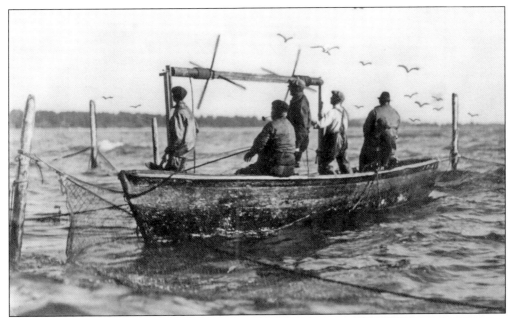

Pictured here is a typical commercial fishing operation in Lake Michigan near Milwaukee. Note the hand pulleys used to lift the pot of the pond net, thus pulling the whitefish and other species into the boat. The catch often consisted of sturgeon, perch, bass, trout, and whitefish, most of which went to the Whitefish Bay Resort. (Courtesy of the Milwaukee County Historical Society.)

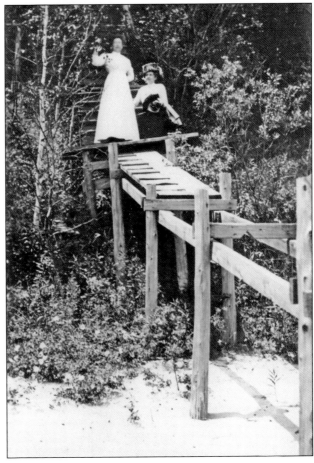

Two ladies look out from the steps leading to the fishing pier used by Lewis Scheife, and later by Pete Schaefer, for their fishing enterprise. Scheife furnished all of the fish for the Whitefish Bay Resort, from 300 to 600 pounds weekly. He also had a regular route to deliver fish by wagon twice a week to wealthy eastside residents.

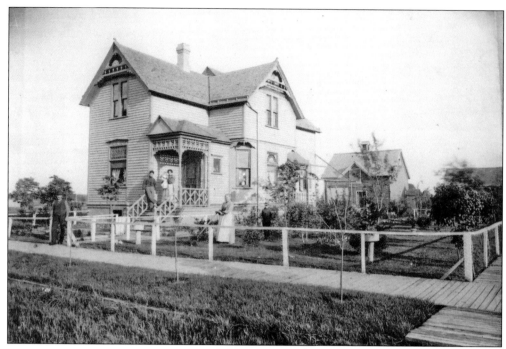

This well-maintained farmstead was built in 1894 for Joseph and Minnie Julien on the southeast corner of East Henry Clay Street (then named Washington Avenue) and present Elkhart Avenue (which did not exist then). This photograph is courtesy of Olive Julien Schroder, a granddaughter of Joseph and Millie Julien. Schroder was born in 1896 and is pictured in her mother's arms in this photograph.

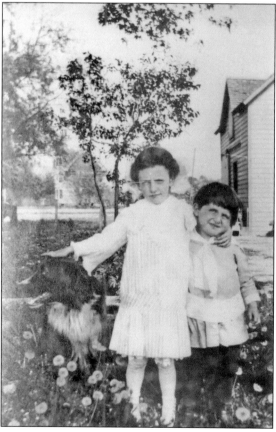

This photograph from the early 1900s shows the Julian children and a dog in the yard of their grandparents' house (shown in the previous photograph). The view looks east toward the southeast corner of present Woodruff Avenue and Henry Clay Street. Catherine Taufner's house is shown in the background. Taufner's house was built in 1894 on the west side of the Chicago and Northwestern railroad tracks.

Lydia Runge poses at the home of her maternal grandparents, Philip and Dora (Rose) Mohr, around 1915. The small child's name is unknown. The dirt road on the right side of this photograph is Henry Clay Street. The Mohrs were among the earliest settlers of the village. Philip Mohr farmed 20 acres just north of Henry Clay Street and east of Lydell Avenue.

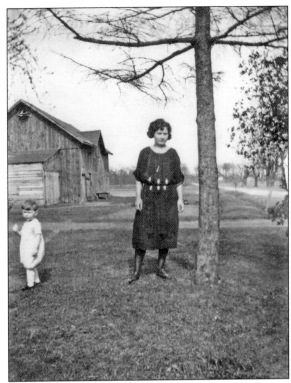

Unnamed workers harvest produce from the Mohr farm field. The census lists the Mohrs as vegetable gardeners. Philip Mohr's obituary reported that he used to help his father bring farm produce and wood to the market in Milwaukee via ox-drawn cart. It was necessary to ford the Milwaukee River at a spot in what is now Lincoln Park. The market was located in Milwaukee's City Hall Square.

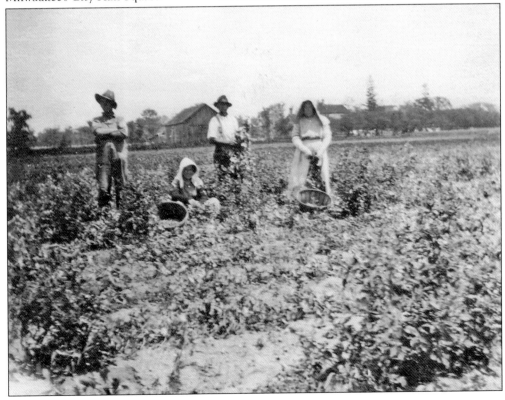

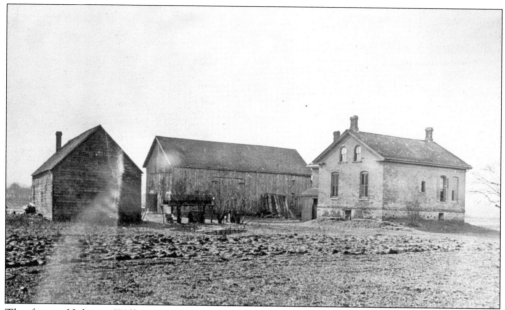

The farm of Johann William Geilfuss and his wife, Louisa (Koenig), was located on the south side of East Silver Spring Drive near the current intersection with Bay Ridge Avenue. The early log house with chimney can be seen on the left side of the photograph. Johann sold cabbage in the area. The family also owned land on the north side of Silver Spring Drive. (Courtesy of Carl E. Geilfuss.)

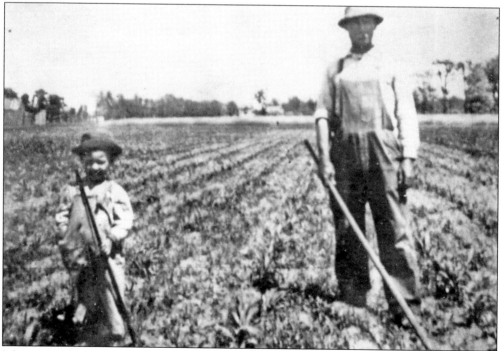

Johann Geilfuss's son Fredrick (right) and Fredrick's son Carl (left) stand in their field immediately south of Silver Spring Drive. This c. 1916 view is looking east toward the present Kent Avenue. (Courtesy of Carl E. Geilfuss.)

This house at 716 East Lake Drive, built for William Consaul, may be the oldest surviving house in Whitefish Bay. Portions of the house exhibit the original plank siding. The Consaul family was among the earliest known residents of the area. Their farmland occupied approximately 35 acres, extending west from Lake Michigan to present day Santa Monica Boulevard, and from Silver Spring Drive north to Lake View Avenue. It is believed that the home was built in 1856.

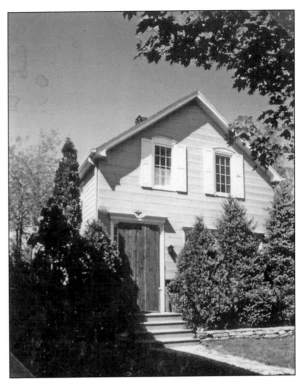

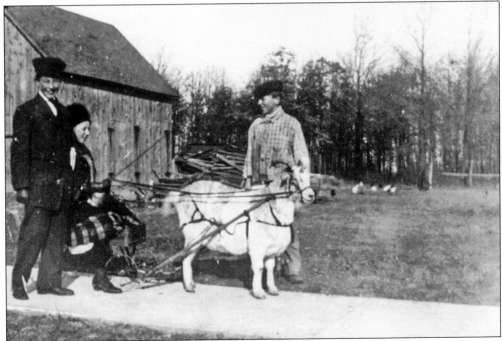

The author has been unable to identify the children pictured with this goat cart. It is known, however, that photographers would go around the Milwaukee area with goat carts, locate children playing outside and pose them, and then ring the doorbell of the home. What parent could resist paying for a picture of their children playing with a goat cart?

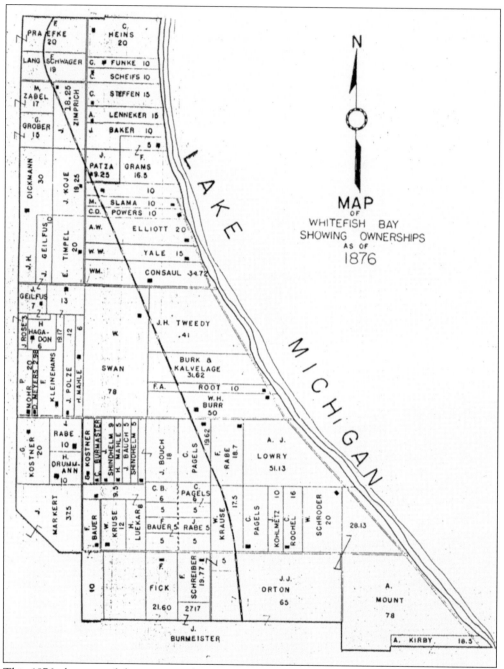

This 1876 plat map of the area now known as Whitefish Bay shows the property ownership at that time.

Two

Transportation and Resorts

While relatively close to the city of Milwaukee, there were no good transportation choices to get to and from the Whitefish Bay area in the early 1800s. Travelers could follow the old Sauk Indian Trail, but it was narrow and often inaccessible due to mud in wet weather. Neither Lake Michigan nor the Milwaukee River were navigable during the winter months. As a result, no reliable route was available for bringing farm products to market in the city, or for city folk that wanted to visit the area.

This ended when the earliest road was built. In 1869, Charlie Andrews, proprietor of the Newhall House in Milwaukee, formed the Lake Avenue Turnpike Company and obtained a state charter to operate a toll road. Built at a cost of $50,000, the new road was opened in the fall of 1872.

John Luck saw the new road as an opportunity and opened a small tavern near its north end in Whitefish Bay. Others soon took advantage of the setting for taverns and resorts, including the Pabst Brewing Company which built the Whitefish Bay Resort in 1889. The Pabst resort was a popular destination and included a beer garden, bandstand, Ferris wheel, the Belleview Pavilion and other attractions. While the resort did not permit dancing, the nearby Jefferson Park dance hall accommodated that activity.

A large pier was constructed at the Whitefish Bay resort. People came via the *Bloomer Girl*, *Chequamegon*, or *Eagle* steamships, which brought travelers from downtown Milwaukee.

The resorts contributed to the local fishing industry. Lewis Scheife began furnishing the Whitefish Bay Resort with 300 to 600 pounds of fish weekly. He also sold fresh fish by wagon twice a week to wealthy eastside residents in Milwaukee.

In 1874, the Milwaukee, Lake Shore, and Western (MLS&W) Railway, built a rail line through the area. In 1886, Guido Pfister and associates formed a separate railroad system, the Milwaukee and Whitefish Bay, better known as the dummy line.

The dummy line brought visitors from Milwaukee to the front door of the Pabst Whitefish Bay Resort, and continued north to Day Avenue in Whitefish Bay. The dummy line continued to serve the area until the Milwaukee Electric Railway and Light Company extended its service to Whitefish Bay and took over the route.

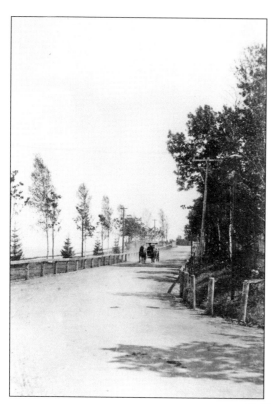

A horse-drawn wagon travels north on the Lake Avenue Turnpike. Built at a cost of $50,000, the toll road was opened in the fall of 1872. C. N. Caspar Company's 1904 *Guide to Milwaukee* called the road, "one of the most beautiful drives of our great country, following the shore for over five miles, giving glimpses through the trees of the limpid water and by turns embowered by the great arching oaks and elms."

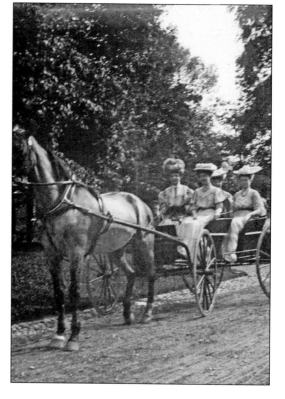

Four ladies, all decked out in their Sunday best, including fancy headwear, travel along the Lake Avenue Turnpike. The improved pavement for this roadway was apparently of macadam. Such roadways typically consist of three layers of stones laid on a crowned subgrade with the top layer being of fine stones so that it seals the surface. The first macadamized road was laid in the United States in 1823.

The *Eagle* was one of several steam-powered excursion boats that took visitors from downtown Milwaukee to the Pabst Whitefish Bay Resort. In this view, travelers await departure after spending an afternoon at the resort.

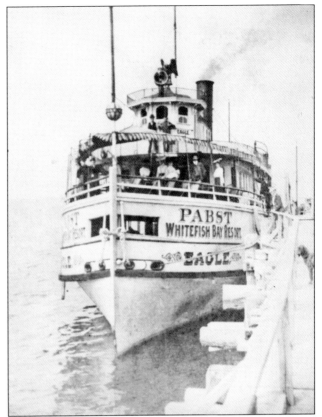

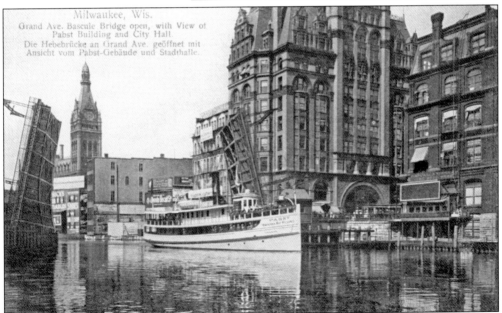

This image of the Chequamegon, from a postcard, shows the excursion boat traveling under the Grand Avenue (now Wisconsin Avenue) bridge. City hall is seen to the left rear of this photograph, while the Pabst Building is the dominant building to the right of the bridge.

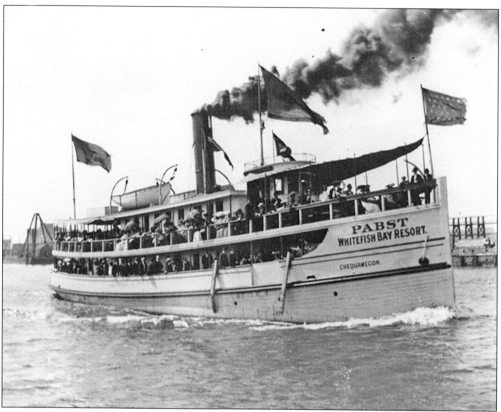

The *Chequamegon* is seen in transit with its decks full of travelers on their way to the Pabst Whitefish Bay Resort.

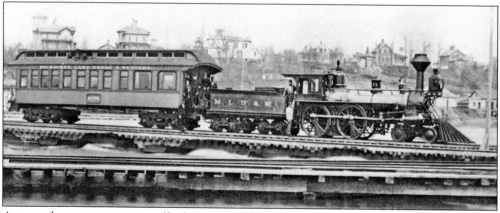

A steam locomotive engine pulls the pay car of the MLS&W Railway. This car stopped at all manned locations on the railway on a weekly basis to deliver pay, and as a result visited Whitefish Bay often. The MLS&W began operating in the area in 1874.

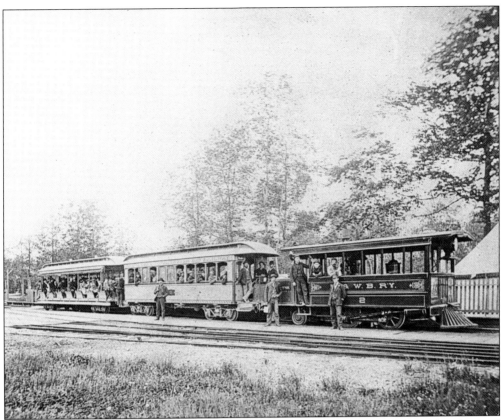
Visible here are the steam-engine-powered locomotive and railway cars of the Milwaukee and Whitefish Bay Railroad. The locomotive engine was surrounded by a car body meant to resemble a streetcar. Such engines were often referred to as steam dummies, leading to the railroad's informal name of the dummy line. Such trains were typically selected because they were suitable for short passenger trips, requiring a small engine to haul a few passenger cars.

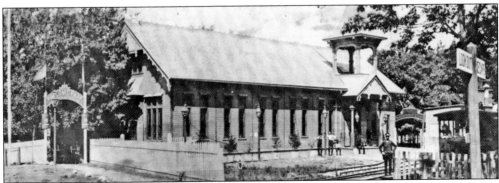
This is the train station that greeted passengers of the dummy line, adjacent to the Pabst Whitefish Bay Resort. It was located in what was known as Welcome Park, just east of the Resort.

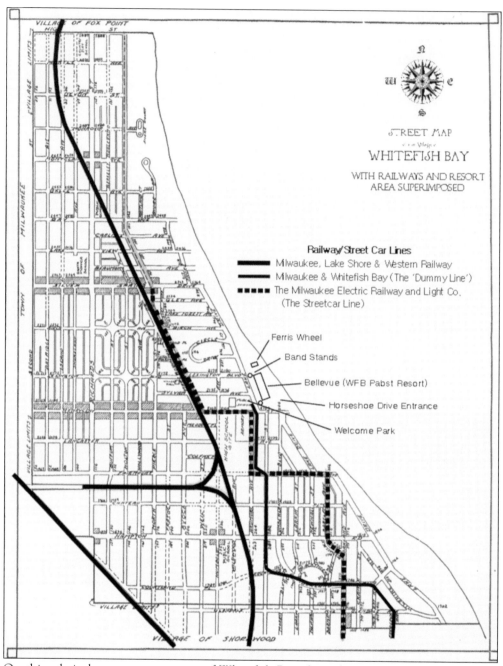

On this relatively current street map of Whitefish Bay, the railways and streetcar lines that once served the village are superimposed. Also shown is the approximate location of the Pabst Whitefish Bay Resort and Welcome Park.

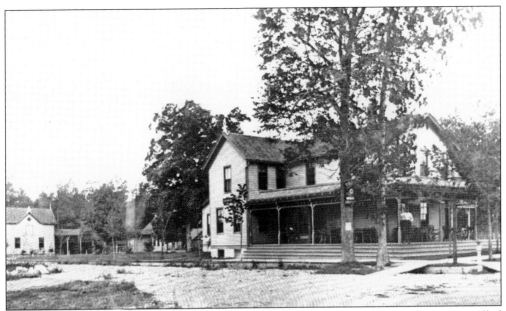

Dr. Williams, one of the founders of the village and its second president, built a resort called Fernwood Cottage on the north side of what is now Lexington Blvd. In 1886 he leased it to Fred Isenring who operated the resort for many years. He eventually sold it to Pabst, which renamed it the Edgewood Family Resort. It was used to house the staff needed to operate the Pabst WFB Resort.

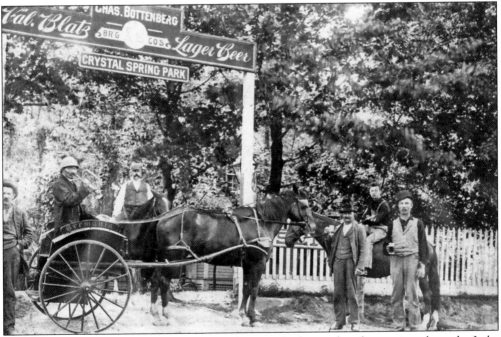

Several men pose at the entrance to Crystal Spring Park, another destination along the Lake located just north of Whitefish Bay in what is now Fox Point. Note the horse drawn wagon with the "Germania" sign, and the helmeted rider displaying a bugle. The Valentin Blatz Brewing Company was incorporated in 1889 and by 1890 was Milwaukee's third largest brewery.

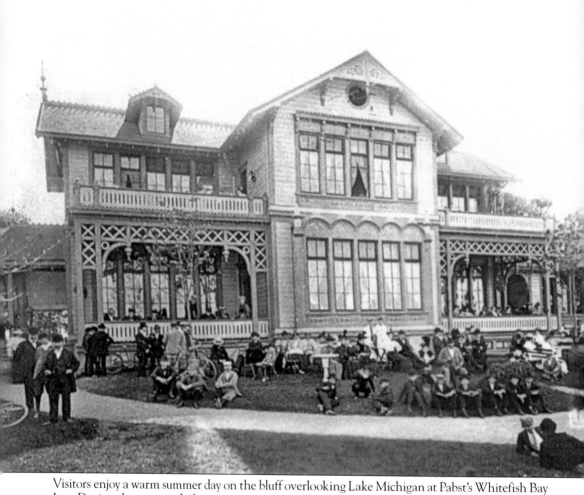

Visitors enjoy a warm summer day on the bluff overlooking Lake Michigan at Pabst's Whitefish Bay Inn. During the season, daily concerts were given by the Joseph Clauder Brass Band outside, and Clauder's quintet inside under the direction of violinist Herman Kelbe. C. N. Caspar Company's 1904 *Guide to Milwaukee* stated that, "rarely do visitors come to Milwaukee who do not spend at

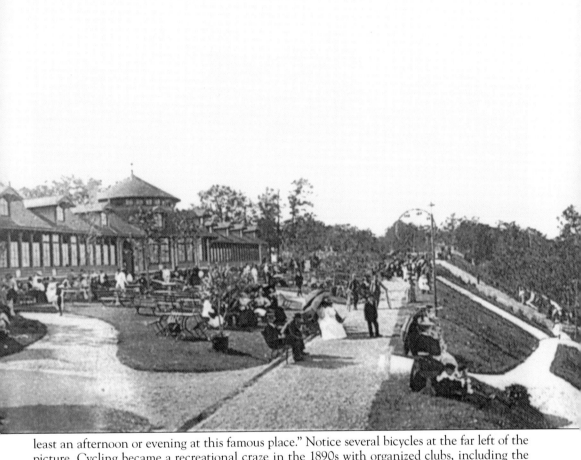

least an afternoon or evening at this famous place." Notice several bicycles at the far left of the picture. Cycling became a recreational craze in the 1890s with organized clubs, including the Wisconsin division of the League of American Wheelmen. To the right of the picture, Pabst's Ferris wheel (described more fully on the next page) can be seen.

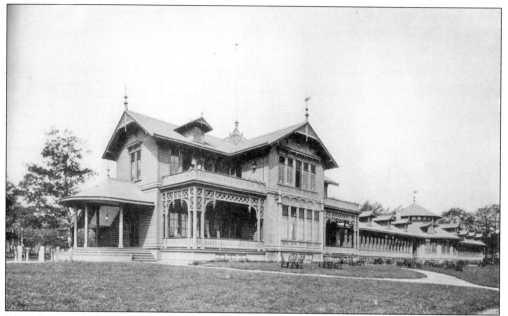

This photograph from *Milwaukee: 100 Photogravures* is the Bellevue Pavilion at Pabst's Whitefish Bay Inn, looking northwest. The ladies' lounge was located on the first floor at the southern end of the building. The dining room was located upstairs, above the lounge. The circular turret to the right capped the bar.

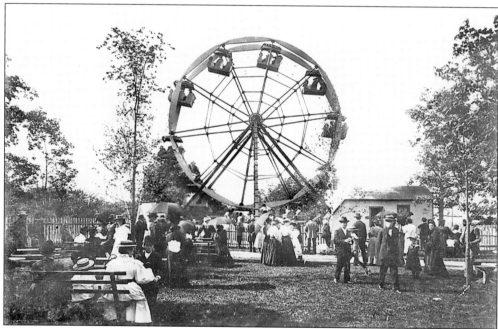

The Ferris wheel at the Pabst Whitefish Bay Resort. The Ferris wheel was popularized at the Chicago World's Fair—the Columbian Exposition—held in 1893 to celebration of the 400th anniversary of Columbus's discovery of America. The Chicago Ferris wheel could carry as many as 2,000 passengers. This Whitefish Bay rendering was obviously very modest by comparison. The Ferris wheel was only one of numerous attractions both on and adjacent to the resort grounds.

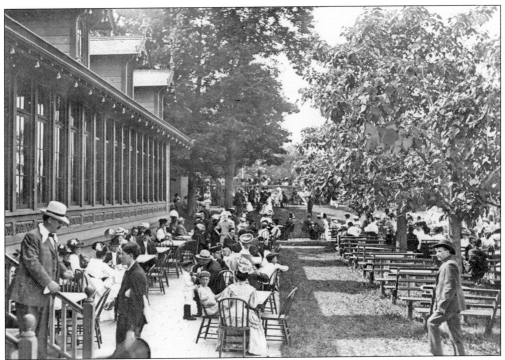

Patrons at the Pabst Whitefish Bay Resort are dressed in their Sunday best. Notice the fancy headwear for women and men alike. Two children with balloons, which must have been a real novelty in the 1890s, are also visible. At left, a busboy takes an order from the customer descending the stairwell. (Courtesy of the Milwaukee Public Library Historic Photo Collection.)

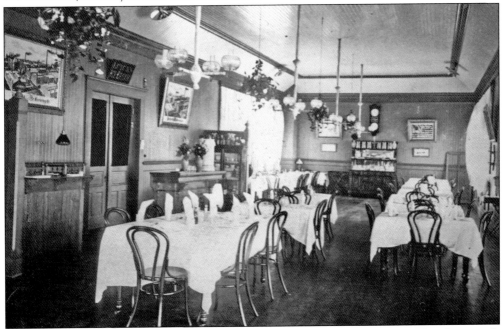

Pictured is a portion of the dining room at the Pabst Whitefish Bay Resort. The photograph hanging on the wall at the far left of the picture is of Pabst's brewery in Milwaukee.

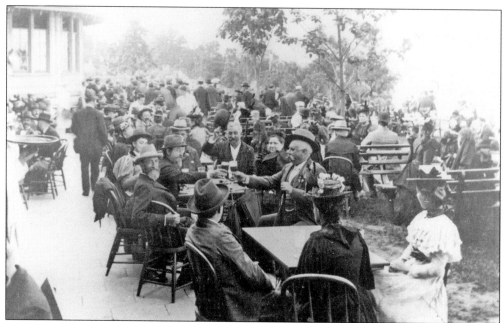

In 1909, Colonel Gustave Pabst hosted a luncheon at the resort for the visiting Ancient and Honorable Artillery Company of Massachusetts. Attendees included Milwaukee mayor David Rose, August Uihlein, Otto Falk, Charles Pfister, John Beggs, Fred Vogel, Albert Trostel, Louis Auer, Edward Hackett, John Kopmeier, and D. W. Herzog, among others—essentially all of the movers and shakers of the city of Milwaukee. (Courtesy of the Milwaukee Public Library Historic Photo Collection.)

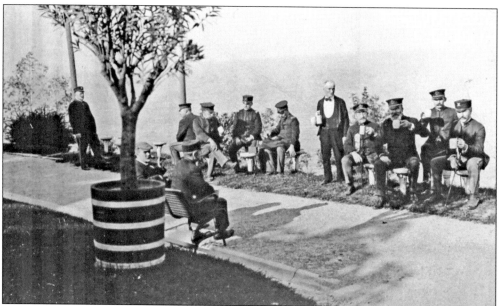

Shown are members of the Ancient and Honorable Artillery Company of Massachusetts, enjoying beverages by Pabst while relaxing on the bluff outside of the Pabst Whitefish Bay Resort. The Massachusetts Artillery Company, which continues to function, is the oldest chartered military organization in North America and reportedly the third oldest in the world.

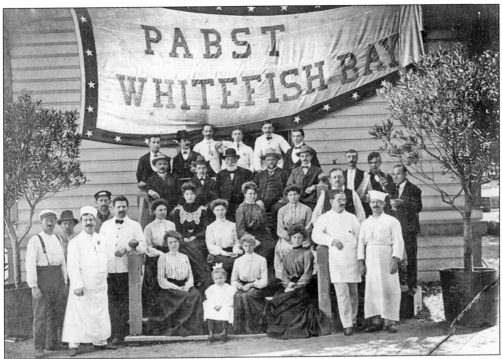

Members of the resort staff pose outside of the Pabst Whitefish Bay Resort. It is believed that Fred Isenring, who operated the resort under lease from Pabst for a number of years, is pictured in the back row, second from the left. Notice the resort's sommelier pictured at the far right, posing with a bottle and glass of wine.

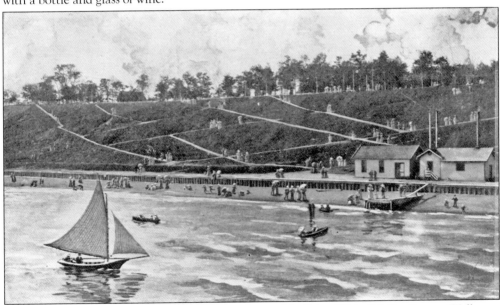

This interesting image shows the waterfront in front of the Pabst Whitefish Bay Resort. Walkways crisscrossed the bluff and provided ample opportunity to promenade. In the days before air-conditioning, a visit to the resort must have afforded a nice respite from the warm weather. (Photograph courtesy of the Milwaukee Public Library Historic Photo Collection)

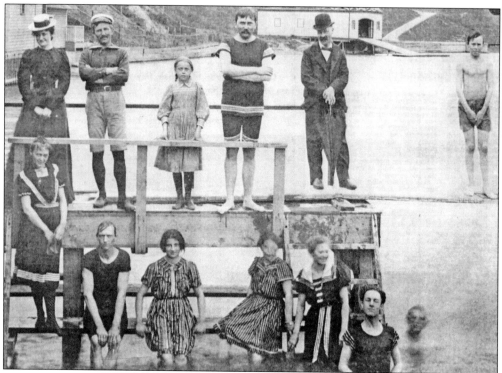

A mixed group of swimmers and onlookers pose for a photograph on the swimming pier at the Pabst Whitefish Bay Resort. It is interesting to note the bathing suits that were fashionable at beginning of the 20th century.

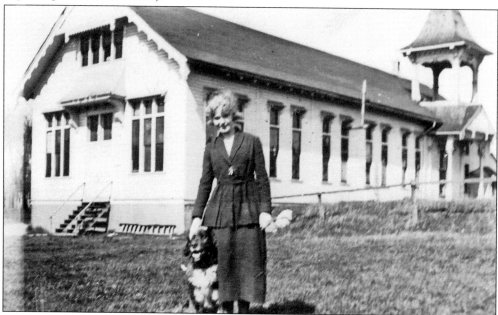

The Welcoming Park train station and pavilion was built just west of the Pabst WFB Resort. After the resort closed, it was moved across Henry Clay Street onto the grounds of the National Guard Armory, where it was used as a drill hall. (Courtesy of George Park.)

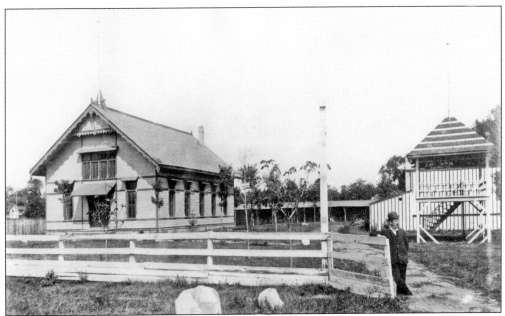

Jefferson Park Pavilion, shown in this photograph, was located just west of the Welcoming Park train station—on the site of what is now Henry Clay School. It was built as a dance hall, and to accommodate overflow crowds visiting the Pabst WFB Resort. It was also moved to the grounds of the National Guard Armory after the Resort closed. It was used temporarily as a school when the village's first school burned in 1918.

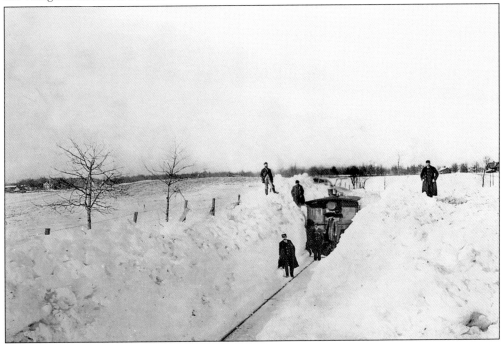

The dummy line train is shown deep in snow on February 19 or 20, 1898. Twenty-six inches of snow reportedly fell during a two day snow storm that winter; reportedly the heaviest snowfall for a single storm in Milwaukee.

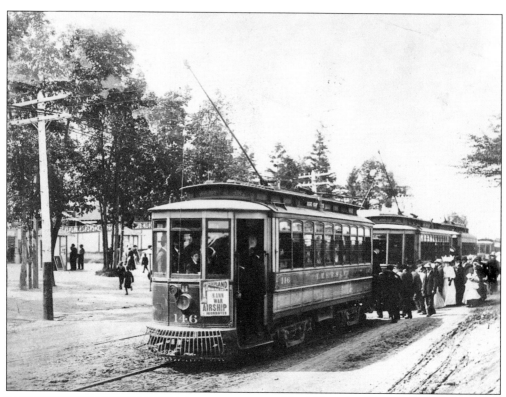

The Milwaukee Electric Railway and Light Company (TMER&L) extended its Oakland Avenue streetcar line north to Silver Spring Drive in 1898, causing the dummy line to cease operations. The lead streetcar is shown advertising Shorewood's Wonderland Amusement Park, formerly known as Lueddemann's on the River.

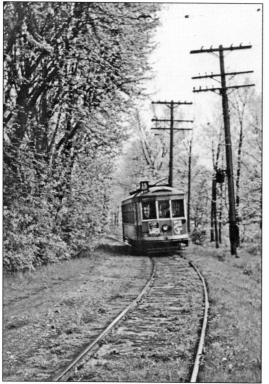

TMER&L's streetcar No. 986 is rounding a bend on Route 15 (Oakland-Kinnickinnic) in 1952, in this photograph by T. A. Carpenter. Electric trolleys began to be replaced by buses in the years after this photograph was taken.

Three

FORMATION OF THE VILLAGE

The children of the earliest settlers—like the Consauls, Markerts, Everts, Rabes, and Grams—had to walk several miles to the Town of Milwaukee School. As the population grew, parents petitioned the Town of Milwaukee Board for a new school closer to the area—but to no avail. George A. Rogers who published a weekly newspaper, the *Whitefish Bay Pioneer*, began a campaign for a village charter so that a new school district could be established. He received enthusiastic support and after several meetings a decision was made to incorporate as a village.

The first step was to prove that the 300 people required by state law lived within the limits of the proposed village. Henry Scheife was given the job of making the official census. Scheife's count completed in March 1892, showed 70 houses and 312 people. A petition accompanied by the census was submitted to Judge Johnson who on May 10, 1892, signed the order bringing our village into existence. Officials were elected on June 5, 1892.

One of the first orders of business for the first village president, Fred Isenring, was to appoint a school committee. The committee prevailed upon the owners of the triangle now bounded by Idlewild, Fleetwood, and Marlborough to donate the tract for a new schoolhouse. The new school building was completed in late spring and dedicated on June 23, 1893. Alice Curtis, the first teacher, received the princely sum of $60 a year (while Nicholas Rix, the janitor, got $75).

After the new school was constructed, the village board met in the second floor assembly room at the school until a building for the first village hall was acquired in 1903.

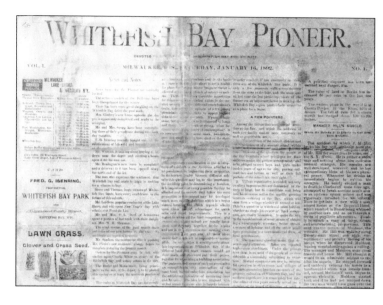

This is a picture of the first edition of the *Whitefish Bay Pioneer* dated January 16, 1892. George Rogers published the newspaper, eventually using it to publicize the movement toward incorporation as a village. While this edition is faded and difficult to read (even in full size), it provides some interesting insights into the history of the area.

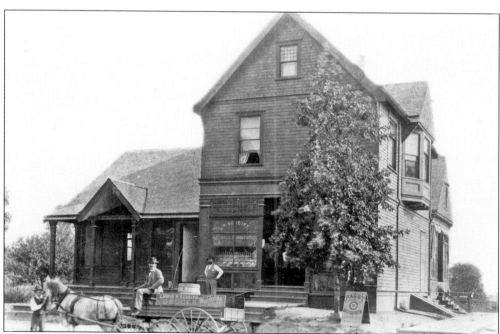

Lewis Scheife's grocery store was located on Silver Spring Drive. In this 1892 picture, Henry Scheife is on the wagon and his brother Lewis is standing. The one-story addition served as a schoolroom until the village's first school building was constructed. It was also used as a meeting place for village officials. Henry Scheife was assigned the task of making the official census upon which the incorporation of the village was based.

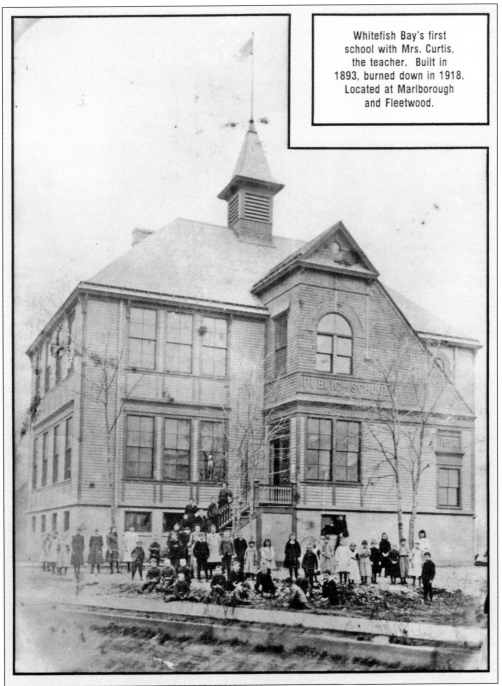

Whitefish Bay's first school with Mrs. Curtis, the teacher. Built in 1893, burned down in 1918. Located at Marlborough and Fleetwood.

This 1893 picture of Whitefish Bay's first schoolhouse is perhaps the most significant picture in the history of the village. The movement to provide schooling for the area children is what triggered the formation of the village of Whitefish Bay. While the building was destroyed in a fire, the site was converted into a park (named Schoolhouse Park in its honor). It is located across the street from the current village library.

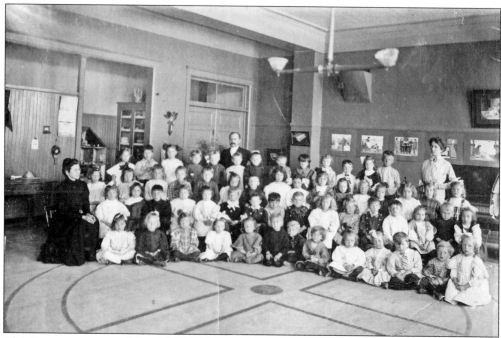

This image was scanned from the original print, which, in spite of its deteriorating condition, shows amazing detail right down to the pictures on the wall. It was taken in a classroom at the first Whitefish Bay schoolhouse. The children are dressed in their best apparel for picture day.

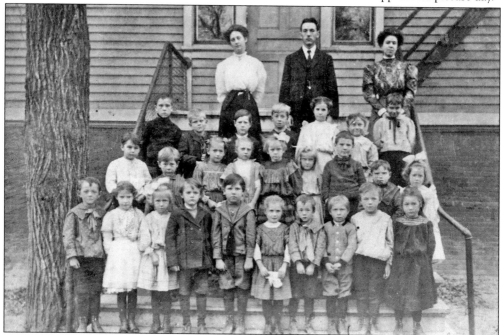

This 1908 photograph, taken at the village's first school, shows Miss Ackermann, Mr. Saunders, and Alice Carncross and their students. Among the children is Lydia Runge (in the third row of children, second from right), who donated this photograph. She was in the second grade when this picture was taken.

Frederick G. Isenring one of the 35 individuals that joined together to incorporate the village. He was also the village's first president, serving from 1892 to 1895. He was active in real estate, insurance, and real estate loans. He acquired a large parcel of land along the shoreline of Whitefish Bay and eventually sold the property to Pabst Brewing Company for the construction of their resort. Upon its construction, he operated the resort under lease.

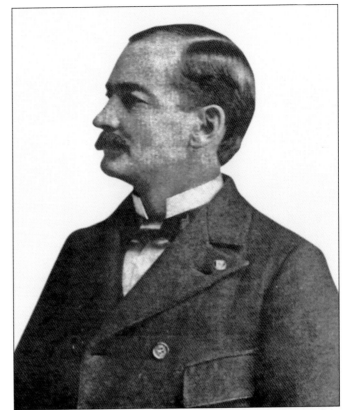

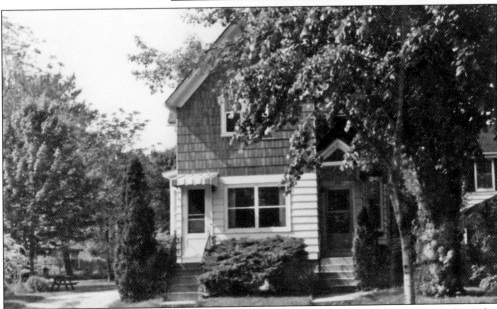

This house was constructed on Fleetwood Place in 1892 for Fred Isenring and his family. A few days before Christmas 1899, Fred Isenring disappeared—possibility because of some irregularities involving county funds. After his disappearance, Dr. Thaddeus Williams arranged to relocate the residence to East Sylvan Avenue. This picture of the home was taken about 1960.

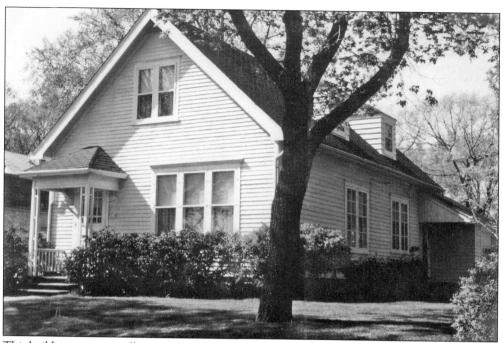

This building was originally erected on the north side of Lexington Boulevard as a saloon. However high license fees imposed by the village put the saloon out of business. The village eventually acquired the structure and moved it to Fleetwood Place to serve as its first village hall. Following this use, the structure was relocated to 314 East Beaumont Avenue where it stands today as an attractive, single-family residence.

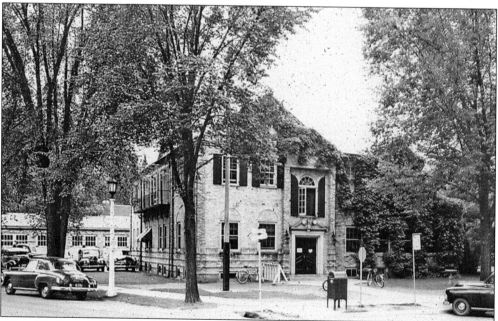

Whitefish Bay eventually constructed a village hall and municipal buildings for the police and fire departments at the corner of Lexington Boulevard and Marlborough Drive. This photograph of the site was taken in the early 1950s.

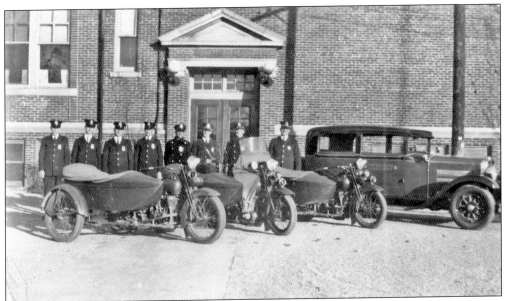

This photograph of the Whitefish Bay Police Department was taken in 1928 at the side entrance of Henry Clay School. Chief George Hage is pictured next to the department's vehicle. The other policemen, pictured left to right behind the motorcycle fleet, are Thorwald Mark, Harvey Sontag, T. Berres, Arthur Priebe, George Nirschl, Charles Miller, and F. McNaughton.

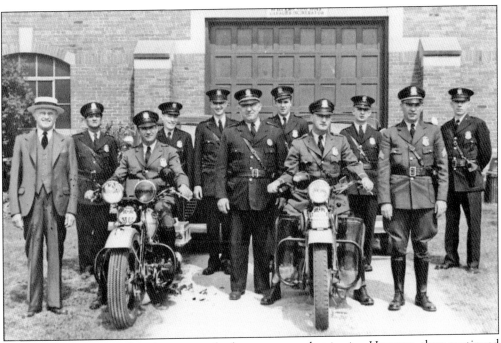

By 1941, the village's police department had grown somewhat in size. However, they continued to use motorcycles for traffic enforcement. Pictured here, left to right, are Charles Weber, George Nirschl, Charles Miller, Thorwald Mark, Dick Schultz, George Hage, Chief Orville Meister, Al Henne, Harvey Sontag, Arthur Priebe, and Roland Rebe.

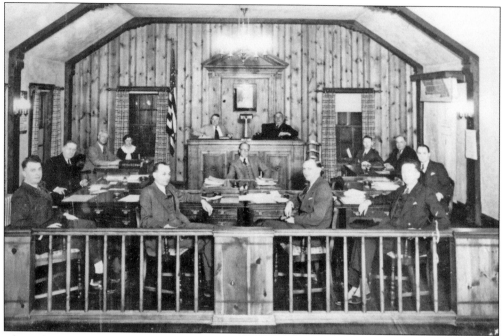

The Whitefish Bay Village Board of Trustees paused to have this picture taken on January 15, 1933. Pictured are, from left to right, trustees Joseph Gallagher and Gilbert Heyer, clerk William Volkmann, deputy clerk Vera Staffeld, trustee Chris Schroeder, attorney George Gabel, engineer Ralph Cahill, president Frank Klode, trustee Thomas Melham, assessor John O'Leary, treasurer Wynand Isenring, and trustees Edward Borgelt and Harold Connell.

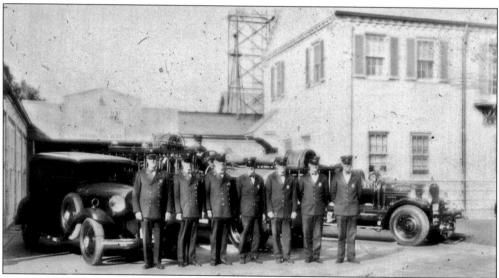

This is another view of the Whitefish Bay fire department, taken somewhat earlier than the cover photograph. This photograph is believed to have been taken in 1936 and it is believed that the eight firemen are the same. Village hall is the building on the right. The fire department's headquarters and garage building is located behind the vehicles. Note the fire tower located on the roof of that building.

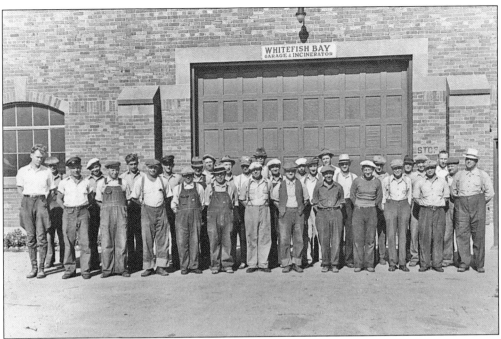

The Department of Public Works employees are pictured in front of the Whitefish Bay garage and incinerator building, formerly located southwest of the intersection of Fairmount and Lydell Avenues.

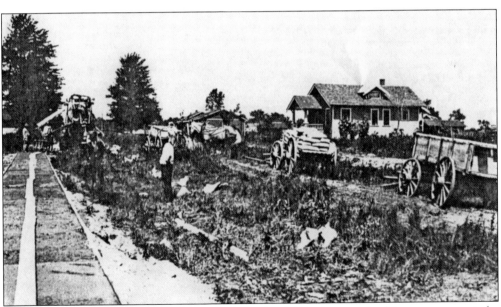

Judging from the width of the forms on the left side of this photograph, this crew appears to be laying new concrete sidewalks in the village. Horse-drawn wagons are shown at right delivering what appear to be bagged sacks of dry concrete mix, suggesting that this somewhat blurry, undated photograph is from the very early 1900s. Note the rural nature of the village at the time of this photograph.

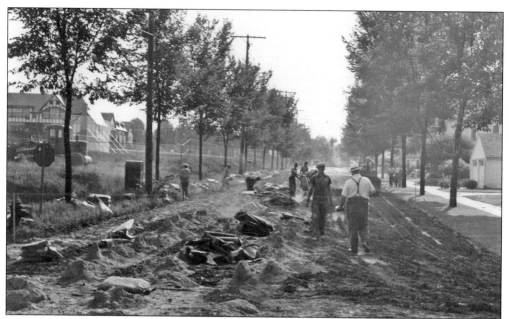

This is a view of road construction on East Devon Street, adjacent to Country Day School (now the Karl Campus of the Jewish Community Center). In this view, the crew is opening bags of lime to be mixed into the soil and compacted, prior to pouring the concrete roadbed. Lime is often added to underlying soils as a stabilizing agent. The year this photograph was taken is unknown but estimated to be from the 1940s.

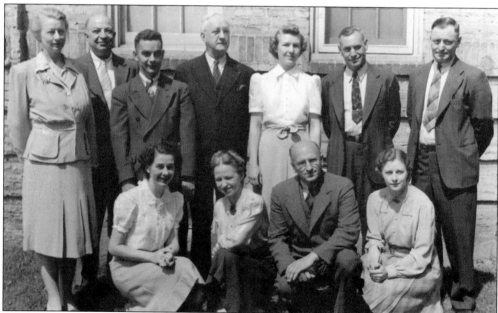

This picture of the Whitefish Bay village hall staff was taken in 1941. It includes, from left to right, (first row) Dora Fritzke, Mary Bowen, Ralph Cahill, and Vera Gross; (second row) Alma Shepard, Tom Buckley, Charles Walker, William Volkman, Lois Dollman, Erwin Pagels, and Arthur Disch. This picture, as well as several others in this chapter, was likely taken in preparation for the village's 50th anniversary, celebrated in 1942.

A water sample is collected in the bay of Lake Michigan, off the shore of Klode Park. It is believed that this sample taking was part of the work that preceded the construction of the village's water intake and pump house in 1961.

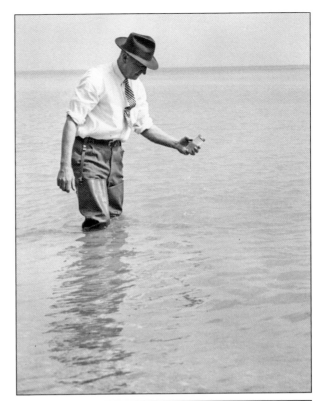

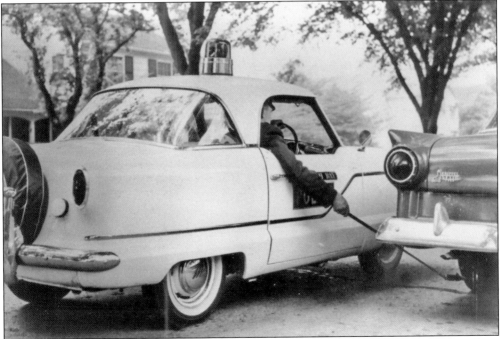

The WFB Police Department used a right-hand-drive Nash Metropolitan coupe for parking enforcement. This picture of an officer applying chalk to the tire of a parked car is from the late 1950s.

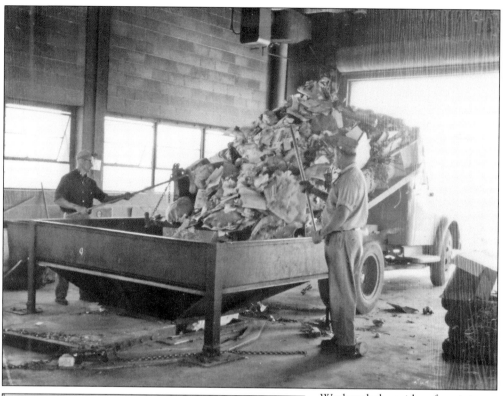

Workers help guide refuse into a hopper that fed the village's incinerator. The village burned the combustible portion of the village's municipal waste until the incinerator was closed in 1972.

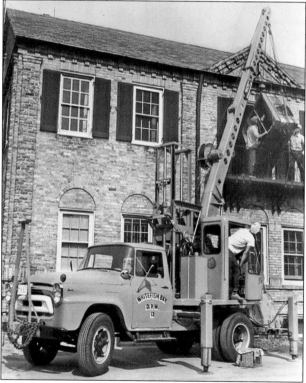

The village uses its Bucyrus Erie crane truck to remove the safe from the old village hall. The current Whitefish Bay Village Hall was completed in 1970. Following its completion, the old village hall and related municipal buildings were razed.

Four

THE RESIDENTIAL HOUSING MOVEMENT

The exceptional location of the Whitefish Bay area—along the lake and in relatively close proximity to the city of Milwaukee—destined it to become an attractive area for residential homes. Once transportation and schools became available, it became desirable to travel from jobs in the city to homes in an area that provided families with a comfortable, community atmosphere.

George Rogers, editor of the *Whitefish Bay Pioneer*, reported in its first edition (January 16, 1892): "No real estate investment is more certain than those in lots of the various plats around Whitefish Bay. One sweet cool breath off Lake Michigan is worth the price of a lot and nothing, absolutely nothing, is charged for the scenery." Perhaps the quote contains a bit of hyperbole, but for a while Whitefish Bay was a realtor's paradise. Nearly everyone wanted to get into the act.

In the 1890s, whole subdivisions were laid out with graded streets, wooden sidewalks, and utilities such as, "Gas, Pure Water and Sewerage" [sic]. A significant number of homes were built near the northern terminus of the dummy line.

Two very interesting homes in this category are known as the Twin Sisters of Lake Drive, built in 1893. These homes are more formerly known as the Henry R. and Marian King Home at 5559 North Lake Drive and the James and Anna McGee Home at 5569 North Lake Drive. At almost the same time, a subdivision was developed in the area of East Day Avenue, and another along East Glen Avenue.

Developers included the first village president, Frederick Isenring, whose real estate activities included the development of three subdivisions within the village. Its second president, Dr. Thaddeus Williams, was also very active in the real estate market.

Of course, housing development was not always smooth. Like most housing booms, the frenetic activity of the 1890s was met with a housing depression in 1898, when the bottom fell out of the real estate market.

In spite of the cyclic nature of real estate development, the village's population grew from 312 people (in 70 houses) at the time of the 1892 census, to 882 by 1920.

DAY AVENUE.

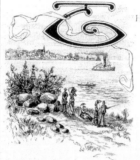

THIS pretty street, in Milwaukee's most attractive suburb, "Whitefish Bay," is two and one-half miles north of the city limits, and within fifteen minutes' ride from Wisconsin street. It is the only street in Milwaukee County, outside of the city limits, provided with Gas, Pure Water and Sewerage.

In 1891 there were only a few scattering farm houses near what has, during the past year, become a village, and as Day Avenue, east of the Milwaukee, Lake Shore & Western Railway, had been provided with such modern conveniences as Water Works, Gas and Sewerage, the best houses were, of course, built there, and this little book is intended to show those who have not been able to see for themselves how this most attractive part of Milwaukee County is being built up.

If you desire to become the owner of a Modern Home, a house supplied with Gas at little expense, and with pure Spring Water for drinking purposes, containing Bath Room, Furnace, and, in fact, everything that should be in a modern house, at a moderate cost and on very easy terms, then do not fail to call on us, for we own desirable vacant property on Day Avenue, which is provided with Water, Gas and Sewerage, that can be had for building purposes.

Whitefish Bay Association,

ALONZO FOWLE, President.
C. R. GETHER, Secretary.

Room 60 Loan & Trust Building,

MILWAUKEE.

This is an early real estate advertisement for Day Avenue by the Whitefish Bay Association. It touts that "it is the only street in Milwaukee County outside of the city limits provided with Gas, Pure Water and Sewerage [sic]" and notes that until "1891 there were only a few scattering farm houses near what has, during the past year, become a village."

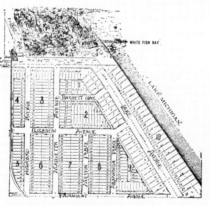

MAP OF HIGHLAND VIEW,
IN THE SOUTH EAST ONE QUARTER OF SECTION 33,
TOWN OF MILWAUKEE.

THIS delightful suburban residence tract is located at White Fish Bay. It is one hundred feet above Lake Michigan, and has seventeen hundred feet of lake front. It commands a magnificent view of the lake and of the city in the distance. The Milwaukee & White Fish Bay Railway runs through this tract on the west, and its depot is located just across the road, affording the greatest convenience for residence purposes, with quick communication with the city.

Bellevue Hotel and Park, owned by Capt. Pabst, join it on the north. The new docks and steam-boat landing are almost directly in front of this property, and boats run regularly to and from the city. Lake Avenue, a macadamized road, runs through this tract on the east and north, and with its natural beauties of scenery, is one of the finest drives in the world.

Parties residing on this property, have the advantages of living on the Bay near the steam-boat landing, on Lake Avenue, and near the depot of the White Fish Bay Railway, advantages for beauty of scenery and convenience which are destined to make it one of the most desirable and popular summer resorts in the country. On the south east of this tract there are a number of mineral springs. The water possesses properties equal to the medicinal springs of Waukesha, iron and sulphur predominating.

The banks along the shore of the lake are composed of a valuable clay, which has by a number of tests, been proven to possess qualities for making fine stone-ware.

Several gentlemen, who have investigated the matter, have become enthusiastic over the prospect of turning this clay to a practical use. For plats and further particulars apply to **I. H. LOWRY, 82 Michigan St**

This early real estate advertisement appeared in a souvenir brochure for the Whitefish Bay Resort. The map shows the location of the Highland View subdivision in proximity to the resort and the depot of the Whitefish Bay Railway. It is interesting to note that many of the current village streets do not align with this plan, and most others have different names.

The images of these three homes appeared in a brochure advertizing the Day Avenue development. They were built in 1892, the year the village was incorporated. Most of these early Victorians have been faithfully maintained over the years. As a result, Milwaukee County named East Day Avenue a historic district. The top image shows the house of C. R. Gether, Secretary of the Whitefish Bay Association, the real estate firm that was developing the area. His home was at 726 East Day Avenue. It originally had a third floor, as shown in this picture, but was remodeled after a fire. Gether was instrumental in getting the railroad tracks extended as far as Day Avenue to help promote the subdivision. The home in the middle image was owned by Alonzo Fowle, president of the firm, and is located at 624 East Day Avenue. Fowle was also the village's seventh president (1906–1908), and a partner in the King, Fowle, Lawton, and McGee Printing Company. Fowle, King and McGee were among the village's first commuters, living in Whitefish Bay and working in downtown Milwaukee.

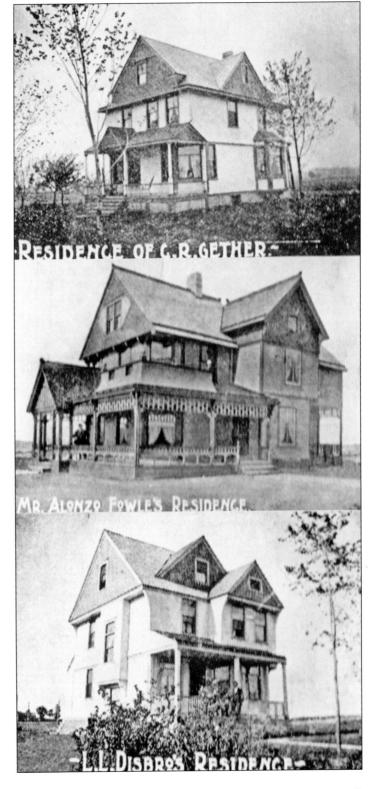

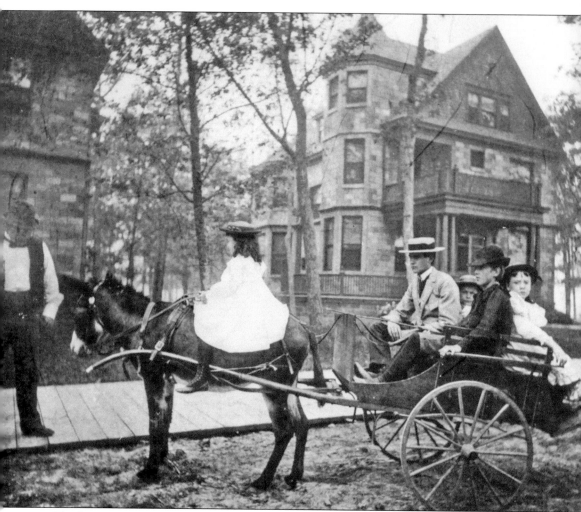

The house pictured in the background (5569 North Lake Drive) is the McGee Residence, one of two homes known as the Lake Drive Twins built for the James and Anna McGee and Henry and Marian King families in 1893. The homes were considered the most elegant residences in the area until 1920, when other large homes were built along Lake Drive. Henry King and James McGee were partners in a nationally-known publishing business located in downtown Milwaukee. Anna McGee and Marian King were sisters and granddaughters of Solomon Juneau, one of Milwaukee's founders and its first mayor. They were also great-granddaughters of Jacques Vieau, a French Canadian and voyageur who traveled by canoe between Montreal and Green Bay. Pictured in this 1894 photograph on a donkey drawn wagon are, from left, Henry King, Pauline McGee (on donkey), Harry King (in straw hat) and his brother, Paul Juneau King. The child between the boys is unidentified; the girl in the back is Helen King. Notice the wooden sidewalk and dirt road that graced Lake Drive at that time. (Photograph and information courtesy of Anson Buttles and the Milwaukee Public Library Historic Photo Collection.)

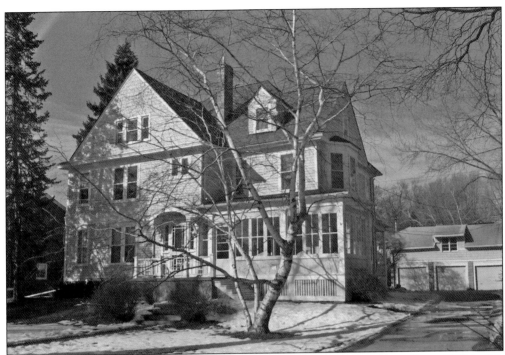

This is the residence of Dr. Thaddeus Williams, the second president of the village of Whitefish Bay. It is located at 942 East Sylvan Avenue. He was also the village's first health officer and was very active in area real estate. He was married (to Alice J.) and had a daughter named Grace.

This residence was originally built for Richard Seyfert. He owned a soda water factory, located near the present alley north of the residence. His main client was the Whitefish Bay Resort. In April 1897, Conrad Cassel purchased the factory and home. Children reportedly would bring empty soda bottles that they found on the Resort grounds after Sunday picnics and return them for free soda.

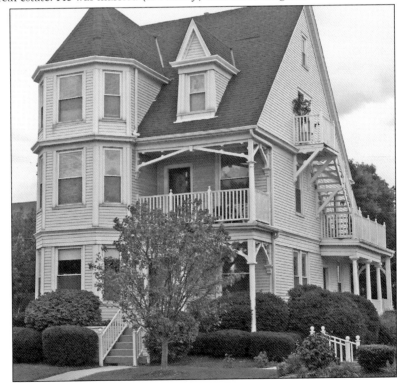

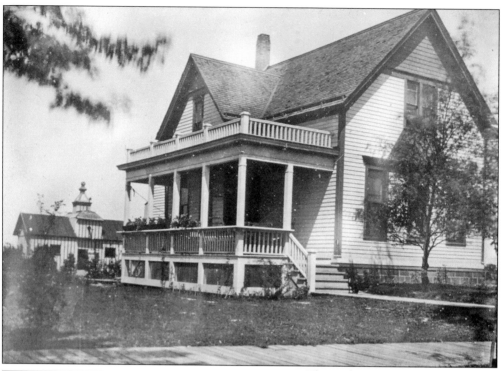

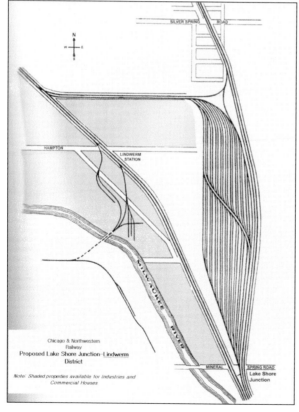

This is the residence of Reinhold and Anna Knop at 5915 North Lake Drive. It was built in 1893. Notice the wooden plank sidewalk in front of the residence in this early picture. Anna was one of the organizers of hot lunches for school children in the village. This task was carried out by the Mothers' Club, which was a forerunner of the PTA movement.

In 1904 the Chicago and Northwestern Railway announced its intention to develop a large rail yard in the area shown in this map, which spans a substantial portion of what is now Shorewood and Whitefish Bay. While never constructed, rumors of the plans may have prompted Milwaukee real estate firm of Stone and Thomas to plat a subdivision in the area—Idlewild subdivision. (Courtesy of The Railway and Locomotive Historical Society and Ray Specht.)

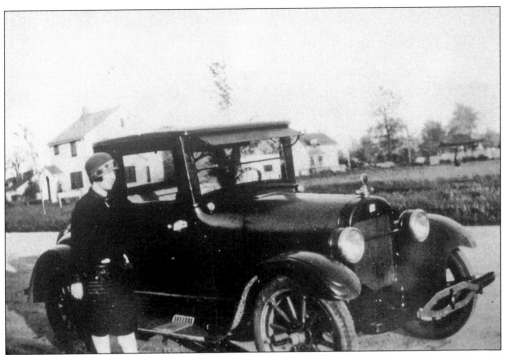

Julia Haupt looks over the site of the new home being built for her and her husband, Howard, at 614 East Beaumont Avenue. This photograph was taken in late spring 1926. (Courtesy of Peter Haupt.)

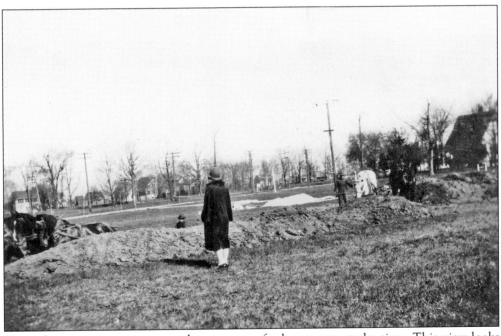

Horse-drawn equipment was used to excavate for basements at the time. This view looks northwest toward Lake Drive with houses in the distance on Lakeview Avenue. (Courtesy of Peter Haupt.)

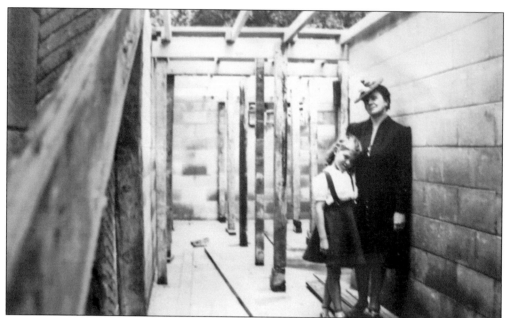

Jeanne Vriesman and one of her daughters tour the work site of her new home at 4800 North Cumberland Boulevard during construction. The home, built for her and her husband, Dar, was a concrete demonstration house. The interior face of the blocks on the right side of the photograph was later covered with 2-inch insulation with periodic furring strips, a moisture barrier, and then plasterboard.

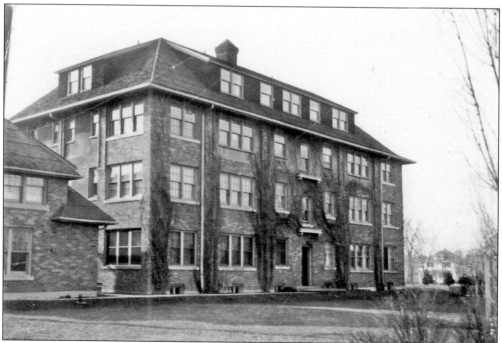

The first apartment building constructed in Whitefish Bay was at 1700 East Chateau Place. While it met with some resistance from neighboring residents, it was completed in 1922. The three-story brick and stucco structure was developed by Ray Tompkins at an estimated cost of $90,000.

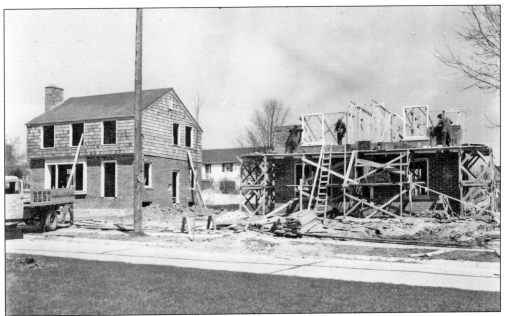

At the conclusion of the Second World War, housing construction boomed to meet the increased demand of the newly released soldiers and their families. The Mickelson Colonial home design was used widely within the village to meet this demand. Two such examples are these homes under construction at (left to right) 6266 and 6260 North Santa Monica Boulevard in late April of 1947.

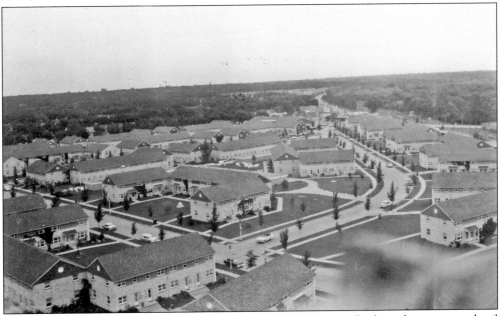

When property formerly held by the Chicago and Northwestern Railway for a proposed rail yard was acquired, it enabled this large area of the village to be developed. Most of the land was developed for townhouses. This view from 1956 appears to have been taken from the top of the chimney on the village's incinerator. It looks southeast toward the intersection of Wilson, Santa Monica Boulevard and Hampton Road.

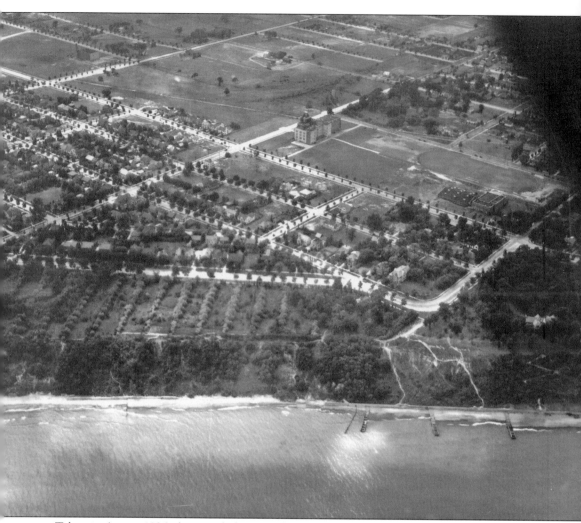

Taken in August 1936, this aerial photograph provides remarkable visual information about the development of the village. In the upper middle of the photograph Whitefish Bay High School can be seen, shortly after its initial construction. Beyond (above) the high school is the property that ultimately became Cahill Square. The remnants of the railroad tracks can still be seen, including the 'Y' that once existed there. Cumberland Grade School is in the upper left of the photograph. The property immediately adjacent to the lake shore, which was yet to be developed, is now Big Bay Park. Palisades Road and the adjacent homes have not yet been constructed. The sharp bend in the road in the foreground of the photograph is Lake Drive and Henry Clay Street. Pandl's restaurant can be seen just west of this bend, and the armory just beyond that. Perhaps most interesting in this photograph is how much of the village west of the lake is still open land, sprinkled with a few farmhouses and barns. (Courtesy of Milwaukee County Historical Society.)

Five

VILLAGE OF FINE HOMES

Whitefish Bay is filled with a wonderfully diverse assortment of attractive homes, with Victorian-era residences sprinkled among a variety of 20th-century architectural styles. The village's proximity to Milwaukee and its location on the shore of Lake Michigan inevitably led it to assume the character of a bedroom suburb, in which most residents commute to jobs elsewhere. By the 1930s, Whitefish Bay became known as part of Milwaukee's "Gold Coast," for the many fine homes located in the village. The village's population, which was 882 in 1920, grew to 9,000 in 1940.

The village has numerous architectural gems that are well maintained and admired. This chapter highlights just a few of the notable examples, which include one of the largest concentrations anywhere of "small houses" designed by architect Ernest Flagg—a dozen such residences grace the village. It also includes more than a dozen residences designed by Russell Barr Williamson, who worked closely early in his career with Frank Lloyd Wright, and a home designed by Cary Caraway, a disciple of Wright.

Also included in the chapter is Judge Joseph Padway's house at 5312 North Lake Drive, designed by architect Hugo Miller; a home designed by architect Harry Bogner at 4725 North Wilshire Avenue—Bogner was a former president of the Milwaukee Art Institute and in 1910 designed their building; the Herman Reel residence at 4640 North Lake Drive, designed by architect Richard Phillip; Casa del Lago at 5570 North Lake Drive, designed by prominent architect Armand C. Frank; several homes designed by notable architects Willis and Lillian Leenhouts; and at least 19 vaulted Tudor Revival homes designed by architects Wesley L. Hess and George A. Kemnitz.

Perhaps most notable of any Whitefish Bay residence is the one built for Herman and Claudia Uihlein, commonly referred to as the "Mansion on Lake Drive." An architectural landmark since its construction in 1919, the house ranks among Milwaukee County's most significant examples of the classical tradition in early-20th-century residential design. It was designed by Milwaukee architects Kirchoff and Rose.

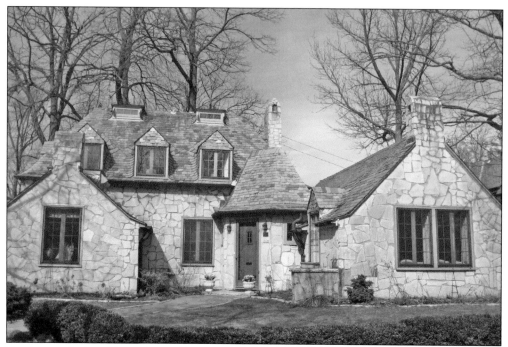

Five homes designed by architect Ernest Flagg are located within one block of each other in the southeast corner of the village. Ernest Flagg attempted to design architecturally distinctive homes that would be affordable for all. They all feature massive stone exterior walls and solid interior plaster walls. This home is on East Glendale Avenue.

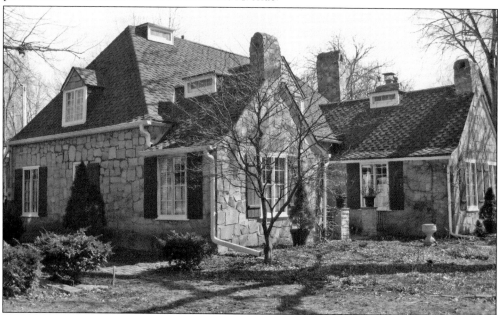

Located just around the corner from the above home is this Flagg-designed house on North Cramer Street. Flagg attempted to maximize the use of space, using the area under roof for rooms that were illuminated with numerous dormers, including his unique ridge-dormers, which were meant to provide both lighting and ventilation.

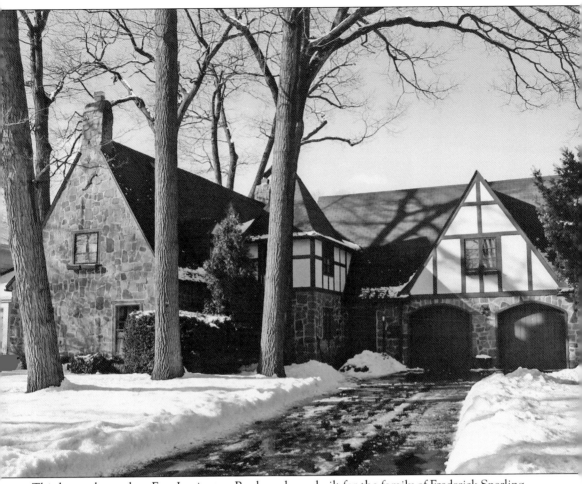

This home, located on East Lexington Boulevard, was built for the family of Frederick Sperling. Like other Flagg houses, the walls were created of stone (in this case Tennessee quartzite) and mortar using a slip-form process. It has four gable dormers and two distinctive chimneys. The square tower encloses an interior stairwell to the second floor. There is a beam and girder ceiling throughout the first floor. This Flagg-designed house is particularly architecturally significant because it closely resembles the house illustrated on plate 15 of Flagg's book on small houses (*Small Houses, Their Economic Design and Construction*). It was constructed in 1924 by Arnold F. Meyer and Company. The Meyer Company built 25 Flagg-designed homes in the Milwaukee area between 1924 and 1926.

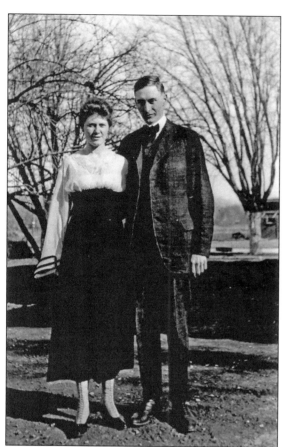

Russell Barr Williamson was a leading architect who designed numerous homes in Whitefish Bay, as well as throughout Wisconsin. He worked for Frank Lloyd Wright and was the supervising architect for two of Wright's Prairie-style projects. Although he worked in a variety of styles, he principally designed Prairie-style homes in the first decades of his career. Here he is pictured with his wife, Nola Mae.

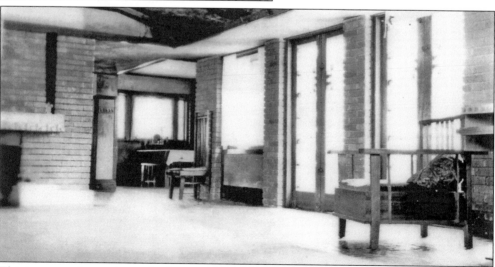

This is a somewhat grainy, early photograph of the living room in the home designed by architect Russell Barr Williamson for his family. It is located on Oakland Avenue in Whitefish Bay. The Wright Prairie-style influences are evident, right down to the straight-backed chairs. The windows and door on the right side of this photograph are leaded stained-glass, also in the Prairie-style, but cannot be fully appreciated by this photograph. (Courtesy of Robin Pickering-Iazzi.)

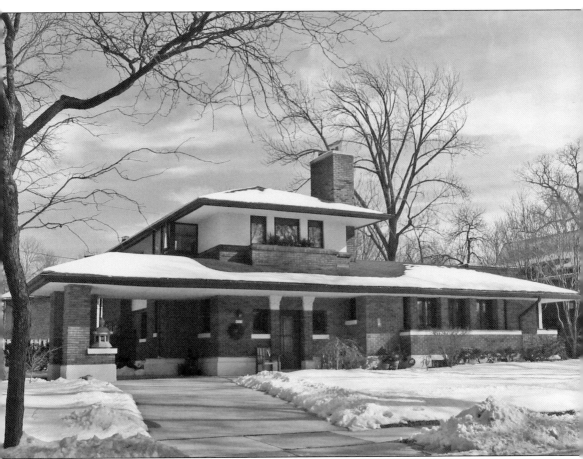

Russell Barr and Nola Mae Williamson's home displays unmistakable influences of Frank Lloyd Wright's Prairie school style. Williamson (1893–1964) spent a number of years working in Wright's firm, before moving to Milwaukee to continue his architectural career, which spanned more than four decades. Their Whitefish Bay home was constructed in 1921. The design reportedly is based on Frank Lloyd Wright's Henry Allen House in Wichita, Kansas. Williamson was the supervising architect for that house while working for Wright, and apparently adapted the design for his own home. Williamson also designed his own furniture for the living room, dining room and sunroom. He and his wife lived in the residence for 30 years and then moved to Oostburg, Wisconsin where he continued his practice until his death at the age of 71.

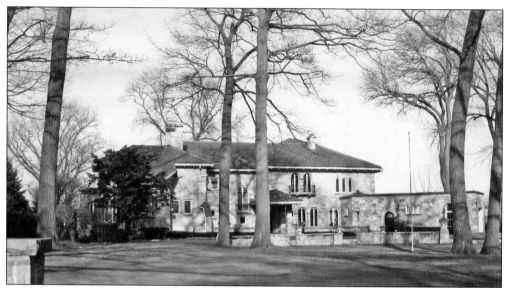

This brick Mediterranean Revival residence was constructed in 1924 for Carl Herzfeld. It sits on a large property (approximately 4 acres) with a bluff overlooking Lake Michigan. It is the largest known house designed by architect Russell Barr Williamson. Carl Herzfeld was president of the Boston Store. The house was also owned for a time by Julius Peter Heil, who was the Governor of the State of Wisconsin from 1939 to 1943. Heil was also founder of the Heil Company in 1901.

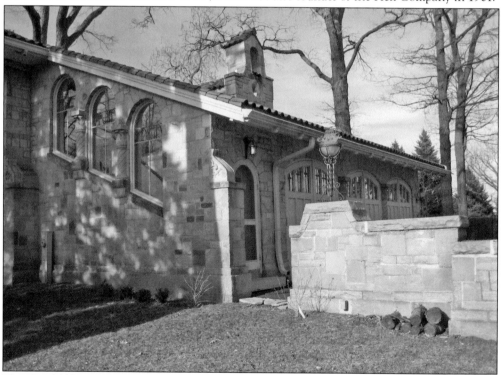

The Herzfeld home also contains an attractive outbuilding, with a garage and an associated coach house. The residence was used as a backdrop in some of the scenes filmed for the 1989 motion picture *Major League*.

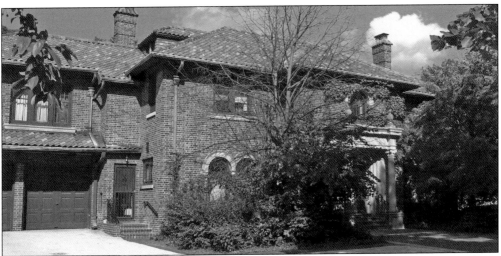

This brick Spanish Colonial residence was constructed in 1931 for Judge Joseph A. Padway. Padway was a lawyer, labor counsel and politician. He was general counsel for the Wisconsin State Federation of Labor and was counsel to a number of Wisconsin unions involved in labor disputes. He won national recognition for his role as counsel during the bitter Kohler Company strike of 1934. The architect of the residence was Hugo V. Miller.

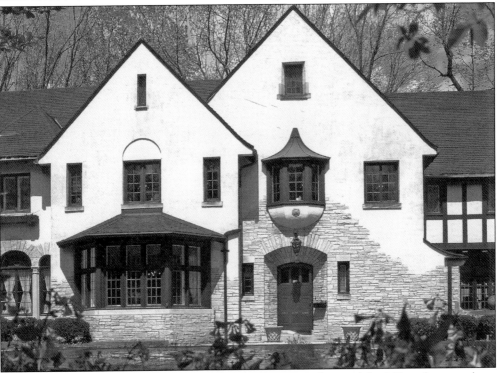

Constructed in 1928, this home on North Lake Drive was designed for Milwaukee merchant Herman Reel by noted Wisconsin architect Richard Philipp. Philipp was the original consultant in the planning of Kohler Village and designed many of its buildings including those now known as the American Club. He, along with Hermann J. Gaul, is listed as the architects for Holy Hill Monastery in Washington County.

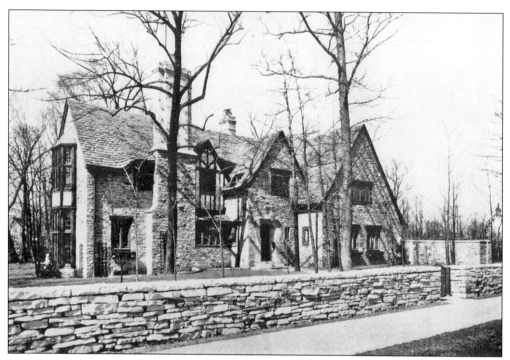

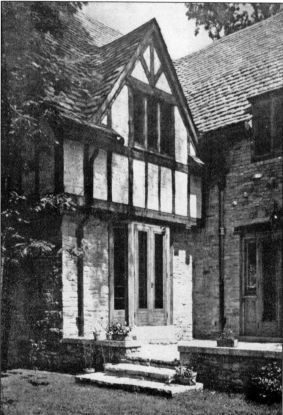

This attractive Lannon stone residence of Tudor Revival style is located on North Wilshire. The house features half timbering at the face of some of the gables, wooden lintels over the principal windows, and a slate roof. It was built for Edward Franz and Erna M. Pritzlaff in 1925 or 1926. The brick and stone residence was originally 2.5 stories with 10 rooms. It was designed by architect Harry Bogner and constructed by George J. Dunn.

This and the previous photograph were featured in *The American Architect* in 1928. Edward Pritzlaff was a buyer for the family hardware business at the time the residence was built. He was born on February 20, 1895, and attended college at the University of Wisconsin, Madison, where he graduated in 1919. He eventually became president of the John Pritzlaff Hardware Company—the largest hardware store in the Milwaukee area at the time.

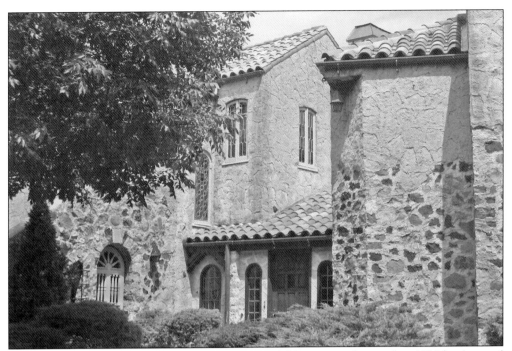

This fieldstone Spanish Colonial, known as Casa del Lago, was designed in 1926 by Armand C. Frank, a leading Milwaukee architect, for his mother, Ella S. Frank. This residence has been declared a Milwaukee County Landmark for its design and outstanding internal craftsmanship. It replicates an Italian villa situated on Lake Como. The house sits on a bluff overlooking Lake Michigan at the intersection of Lake and Silver Spring Drives.

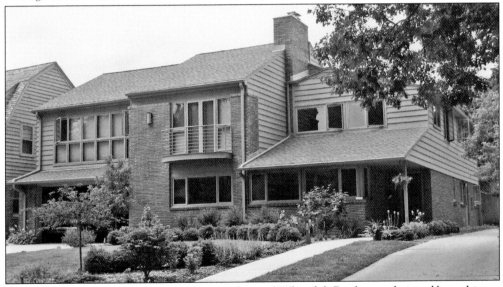

This home on North Maitland Court is one of several Whitefish Bay homes designed by architects Willis and Lillian Leenhouts. Willis Leenhouts started architectural practice in the late 1920s. In 1943 he married Lillian Scott, the first woman licensed to practice architecture in Wisconsin. They are one of the few husband-and-wife teams to be inducted into the College of Fellows of the American Institute of Architects.

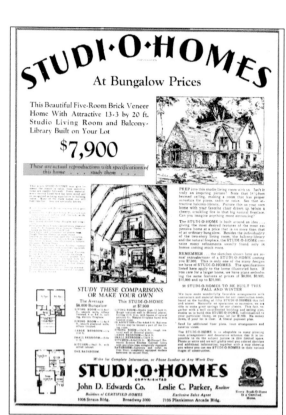

This advertisement appeared in the *Milwaukee Journal* for the Studi-O-Homes in 1928, a design for a Tudor Revival residence that includes a vaulted main room and an overlooking balcony library. The exteriors featured brick veneer and half-timbering. As noted in the advertisement, the design was built around an idea of "giving the most desired features of the most expensive home at the price that is no more than that of an ordinary bungalow."

This home on North Berkley is a typical Studi-O-Home. The initial owners of this well-maintained residence were Harold C. and Marjorie P. Cheetham. The John Edwards Company constructed at least 18 of these homes in Whitefish Bay, all with unique styling. They were designed by architects Wesley L. Hess and George A. Kemnitz.

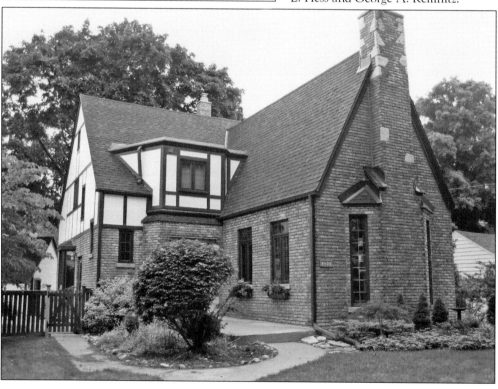

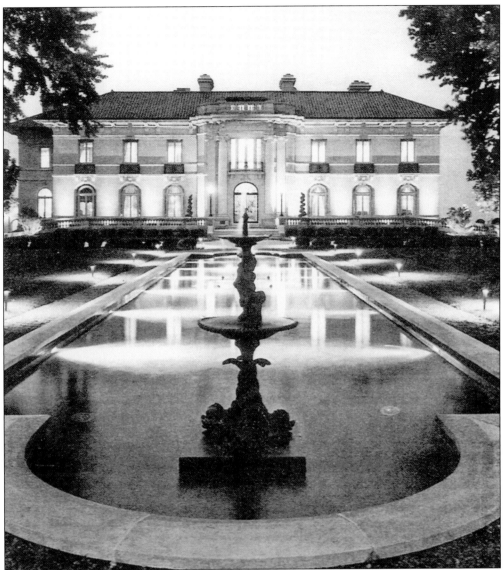

Distinguished by a synthesis of Renaissance Revival and Beaux-Arts motifs, along with a lavishly ornamented interior, the Herman and Claudia Uihlein house is an imposing suburban villa. An architectural landmark since its construction in 1919, the house ranks among Milwaukee County's most significant examples of the classical tradition in early-20th-century residential design. It was designed by Milwaukee architects Kirchoff and Rose. The Bedford limestone from an Indiana quarry was carved on the job site to avoid damage in shipment. The lavish interior was built with 8 different marbles, Caen stone with walnut doors and paneling, and ornamental plaster. The grand sweeping staircase in the main hall has an incredible wrought iron balustrade. The Uihleins, with their four sons and three daughters, lived in the residence with a staff of 10 servants. The house contains nine bedrooms, six-and-a-half bathrooms, five fireplaces, and a detached four-car garage.

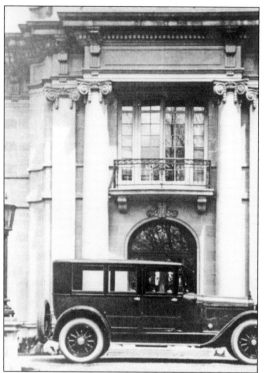

The intricate front doorway grille was designed by master craftsman Cyril Colnik, who reportedly spent three years completing a commission that also included the majestic stairway railing. After apprenticing in Vienna, Colnik came to this country in 1893 to help with the German ironwork exhibits at the Chicago World's Fair. Hearing about the "German Athens" to the north, he decided he could earn a better living as an iron craftsman for Milwaukee's large German-speaking community.

Herman Uihlein was president of Ben-Hur Manufacturing Company of Milwaukee, a firm that made refrigerators and freezers. He was also a director of the Joseph Schlitz Brewing Company and president in the 1930s of the association that sponsored the Milwaukee Philharmonic Symphony Orchestra—forerunner to the Milwaukee Symphony. Here he is shown with his wife, Claudia, and their children. Claudia was a lifelong devotee of the opera and classical music.

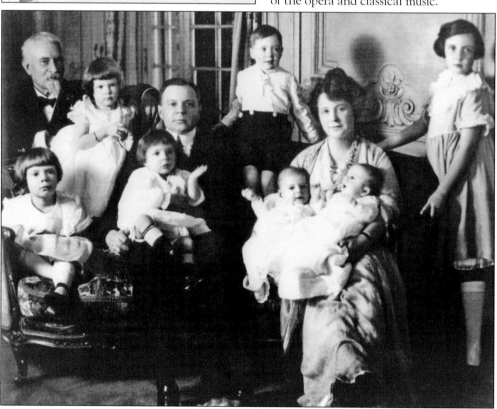

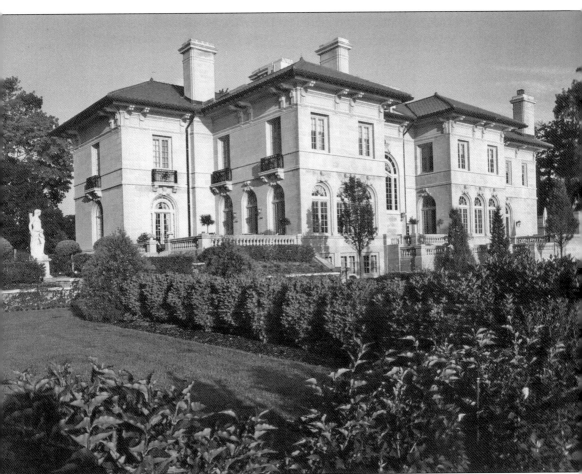

This is another view of the Uihlein residence, looking northeast from the lake bluff. When Claudia Uihlein moved out in 1946, the residence was sold to a real estate holding company. In 1953, the mansion was purchased by the Milwaukee vice-province of the LaSalette Fathers, who used the building as a mission house for five priests and two brothers. In the late 1970s, the Grant C. Beutner family purchased the home. Adding to the significance of the house, the residence was owned for a number of years by Peter and Mary Buffet. Buffet is the son of Omaha billionaire Warrant E. Buffet, who controls Berkshire Hathaway Inc., a diversified holding company. Peter Buffet is a music composer and songwriter. More recently, Dr. Kailas and Becky Rao purchased the residence, carefully undertaking a thorough restoration of the property over the two-year project. Along with the restoration, the entire grounds were improved with extensive gardens, reflecting pool, trees, lighting, and land retaining terracing to keep the property from eroding into Lake Michigan. Great care was taken to update the appearance of the property while maintaining its original grandeur.

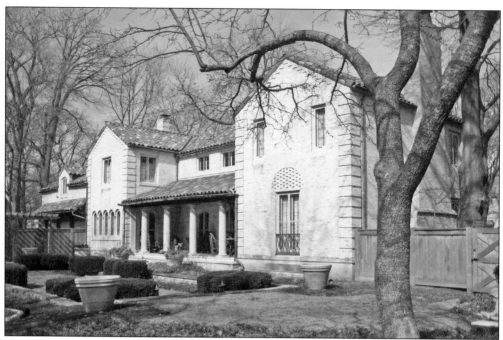

The Wilshire neighborhood is filled with particularly attractive, well-designed homes. This Mediterranean Revival home was built for the family of Melvin Andres, vice president and treasurer of the Andres Stone and Marble Company. The architectural firm of Clas, Shepherd, and Clas of Milwaukee designed it. Clas also designed numerous churches as well as the Milwaukee Public Library.

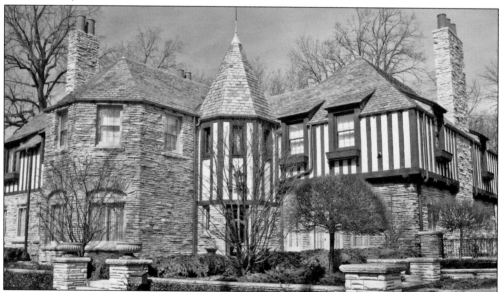

This residence, also on North Wilshire, was designed in 1929 by Milwaukee architect Armin C. Frank. It was built for E. A. and Anita Weschler and their three children. At the time, Weschler was president of Daniel D. Weschler and Sons, a malting firm. The home is designed in the French Normandy-revival architectural style. The home is reported to have a German rathskeller in the basement furnished with an 18-foot refectory table.

Six
WHITEFISH BAY COMMERCIAL DISTRICTS

As non-farm residential neighborhoods were developed in Whitefish Bay, retail businesses soon followed. In the days before transportation allowed residents to move about easily, shops and services needed to be close at hand to meet the needs of the rapidly growing community. Two distinct shopping districts formed in the village—one centered on East Silver Spring, and another one on Henry Clay Street. Both had grocery stores, gasoline stations, hardware stores, banks and other commercial enterprises.

Since the first real estate development activity in the village occurred at the end of the rail line, it is no surprise that the earliest Whitefish Bay businesses also started there. It is believed that the first grocery store to serve the area was that of Lewis Sheife, built in 1892 on land leased from the railroad. It was located approximately where Winkie's exists today. The Chicago and Northwestern Railway tracks ran just to the west of the building. Sheife also served as postmaster. The train would stop regularly to drop off and pick up mail bags. A picture of the store is shown on page 36.

Other retail stores quickly followed. Some continue to serve the community after many generations. Others closed as the nature of retail commerce changed over the years.

Many of the stores on Henry Clay Street have closed and have been replaced by apartment buildings, when the character of the district changed. The Silver Spring shopping district, however, continues to serve the community well with a diverse mixture of retail establishments.

C. SCHMIDT

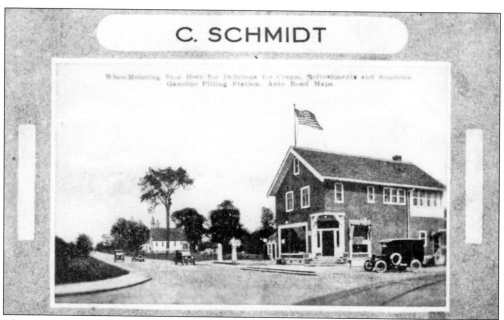

This early postcard shows Carl Schmidt's store—a combination filling station, convenience store, and ice cream parlor. The card urges motorists to, "stop here for delicious ice cream, refreshments and sundries." It was located on the southeast corner of what is now Marlborough Drive and East Silver Spring Drive. The church in the background was an Episcopal church, now the site of Community Methodist Church.

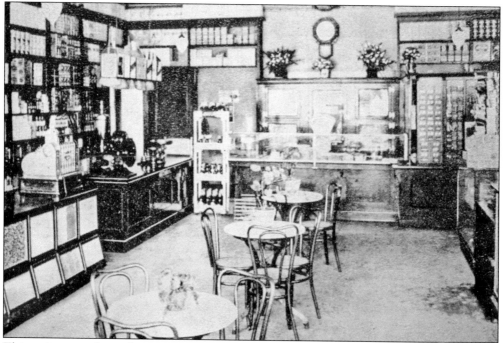

This grainy view shows the interior of C. Schmidt's store, with tables for enjoying ice cream and other refreshments. The photograph was taken in 1917. By 1921, Harold Klann had become the store's owner, renaming it after himself. It was torn down in 1935 for a Pure Oil gas station.

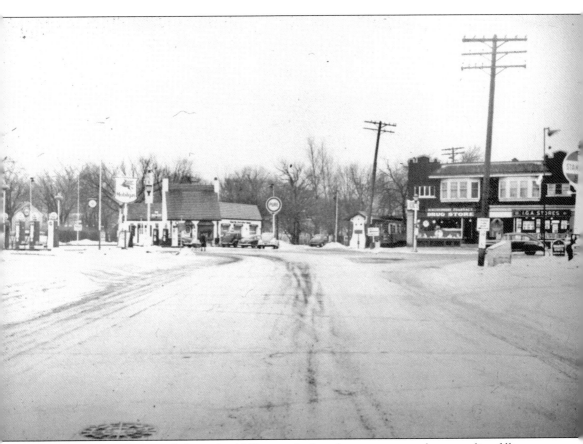

This interesting photograph from the 1940s reveals that there were once three gasoline filling stations located at the intersection of North Lake and East Silver Spring Drives. It also shows the waiting shelter for the trolley line (to the middle right of the picture), located just east of the Whitefish Bay Pharmacy and the IGA grocery store. The building housing these two stores was the second building constructed on this site. It was constructed in 1914. There were apartments upstairs from the stores. If you look closely, you can see a woman pushing a baby buggy across Lake Drive just in front of the pumps of the Pure Gas Station. Marlborough Drive did not extend through to Silver Spring when this photograph was taken.

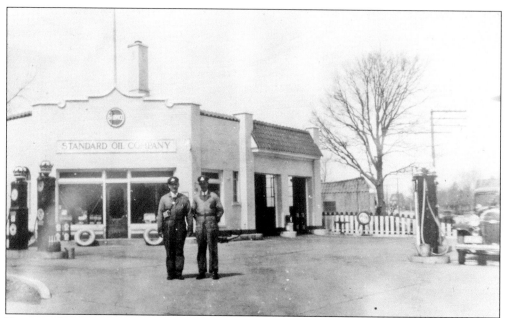

Two attendants stand ready for customers at the Standard Oil Gas Station, located at the northwest corner of Lake and Silver Spring drives. Back then, attendants filled your gas tank and washed your windows while you waited in your car. The man on the left of this 1931 picture is Carl E. Geilfuss (also shown on page 16). Dutcher's Garden Shop can be seen behind and to the right of the gas station.

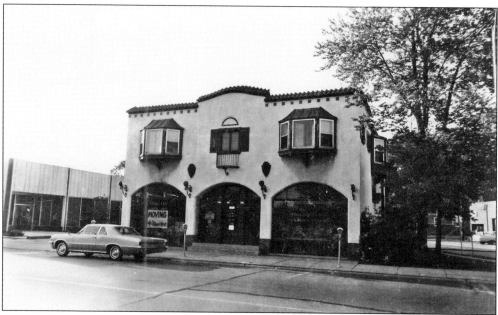

Wilke's Hardware Store was located west of the Standard Oil Station, approximately where Consaul Place is currently located. The attractive stucco Mediterranean Revival store was built by Henry Wilke in 1925. It replaced the previous hardware store, which was a house with a store at the front built in 1899 by Lewis F. Scheife and his brother-in-law, William Consaul. The store was torn down in the mid-1960s.

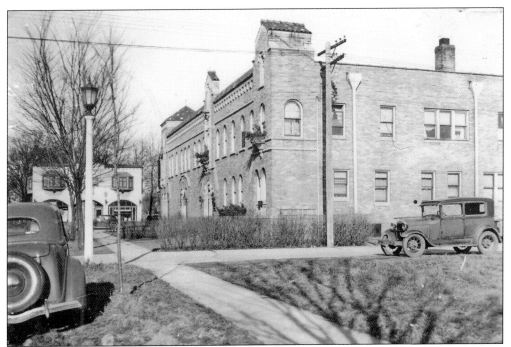

This brick Spanish Colonial commercial building was built about 1930. It features a corbelled cornice, and a square tower on the corner with round arched windows. It was constructed for six stores at the street level and 16 apartments on the second floor. This view looks north toward Silver Spring Drive. The Wilke hardware store can be seen in the background, to the left of the building.

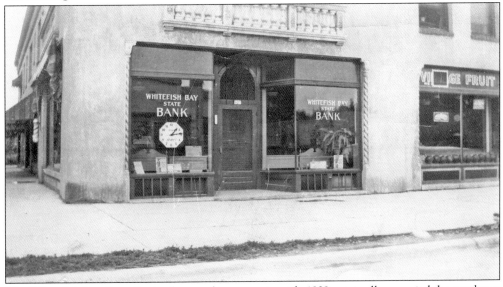

The Whitefish Bay State Bank, chartered in approximately 1929, originally occupied the northeast corner of the Powell Building, a stucco-faced Spanish Colonial commercial building constructed in 1926. To its west, where Bay Bakery is currently located, was the Village Fruit Market. The barber pole of Bay Barber Shop can be seen around the corner. The bank occupied this location until 1942. In that year the bank moved to a larger building, constructed for its use.

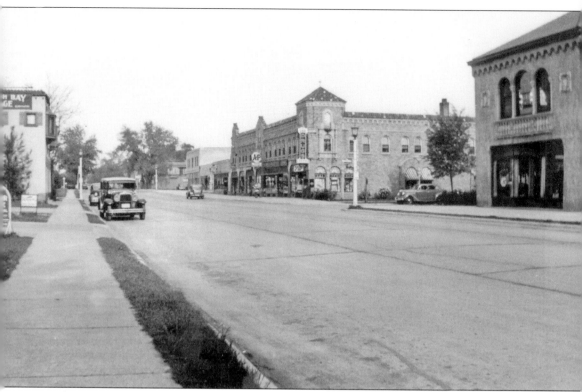

This photograph, which looks east on Silver Spring Drive, reveals a lot about business development along the street. Ott's Drugstore can be seen at the corner of Diversey and Silver Spring, with an A&P grocery store to its east, and a National Food Store just beyond that. The IGA Grocery Store building can be seen a block farther east. (Apparently three grocery stores were located in a two-block stretch.) Wilke's Hardware Store is on the left of the photograph. A sign advertizes the Whitefish Bay Garage, located just to the west of the hardware store. Finally, the Whitefish Bay State Bank can be seen on the right of the photograph. (Courtesy of the Milwaukee County Historical Society.)

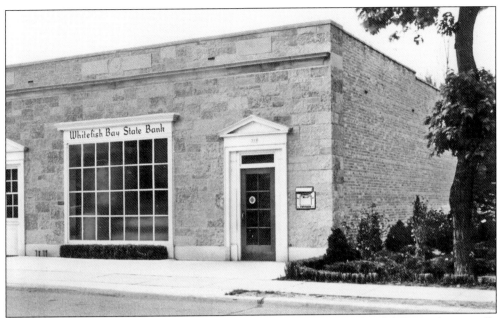

The Whitefish Bay State Bank grew with the thriving community of Whitefish Bay and eventually constructed its own building at 311 East Silver Spring in 1942. The building shown served the community until it was replaced by a newer bank facility in 1958 at 177 East Silver Spring. The bank offered Saturday morning hours, as well as some limited evening hours—both of which were unusual at the time.

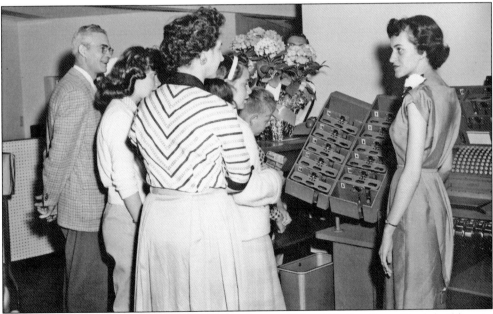

This photograph is from the open house for the new Whitefish Bay State Bank building in 1958. An employee is seeing displaying new check sorting equipment. The Jacobus Company later acquired the bank and renamed it the Heritage Bank of Whitefish Bay, which helped it to increase its business beyond the village. Marshall and Ilsley Bank acquired the Heritage Banking system in the mid-1970s.

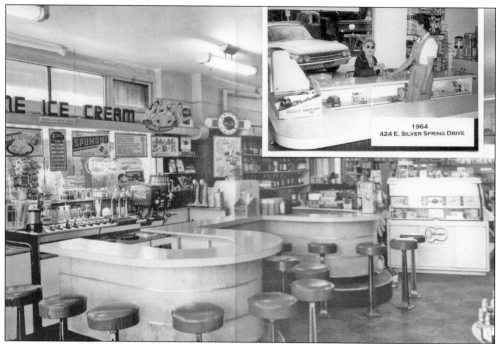

Ott's Pharmacy featured a popular soda counter that offered ice cream, soft drinks, malted milks, and ice cream sundaes. The soda fountain was light green and the clerks wore matching green uniforms. From 1932 to 1955, Florence and Bud Rockwood worked as a team managing the store, which also sold liquor, greeting cards, and sundries. Whitefish Bay pharmacist Dan Fitzgerald eventually acquired the drugstore and renamed it after himself.

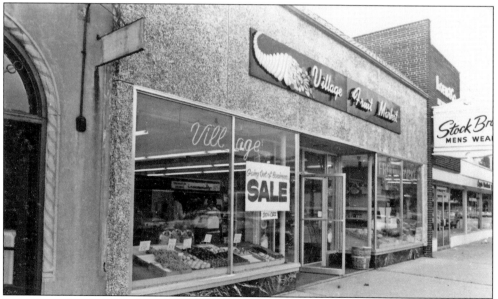

This September 2, 1976, photograph shows the new Village Fruit Market at Silver Spring Drive and Diversey Boulevard. The original store was opened in about 1968 by Jack and Paul Accetta and their wives, Rose and Ida, who were sisters. The family also recruited the help of their sisters Josephine and Janet, as the store's business grew.

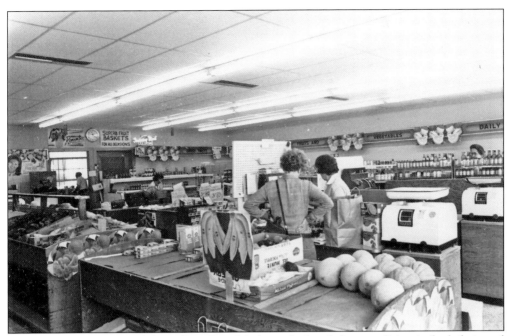

This is an interior view of the Village Fruit Market, which, while specializing in fresh fruit and vegetables, also included other staples, including dairy products and canned goods. The original store was located at the site currently occupied by Bay Bakery. The new store was a stand-alone building, built just to the west of their original location.

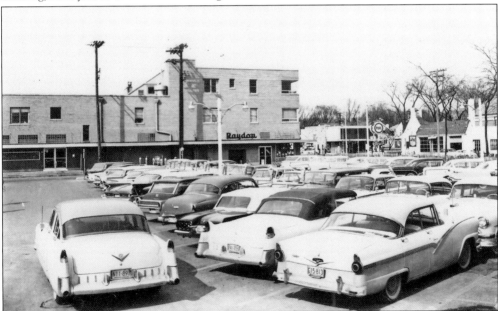

We all recognize this building today as the Winkie's building. However, it was originally constructed for the Raydon Dime Store. It was later expanded to accommodate The Grand department store. Notice the individual parking meters in the municipal parking lot. Also note the Pure Oil filing station with its distinctive style, and beyond it the office building that once occupied the property just east of the northeast corner of Lake and Marlborough.

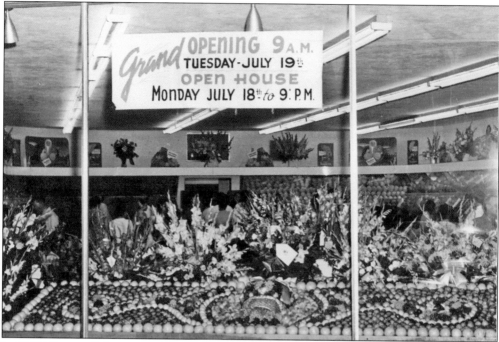

In 1949, Thomas Balistreri purchased property and opened a Sendik's fruit and vegetable market on Silver Spring Drive (his third store). It was colocated with an A&P grocery store. In 1975, the store expanded to include groceries, meat, deli, dairy, bakery and wine and spirits. Sendik's went all out with its window display for its grand opening, emphasizing its fresh fruit and flowers.

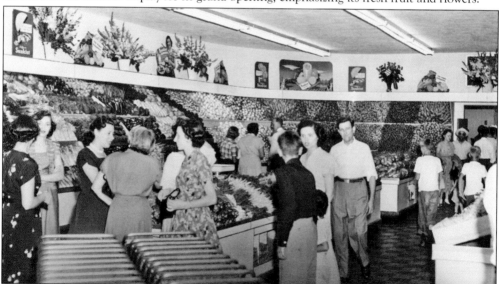

At the 1949 grand opening, Tom Balistreri Sr. (in the white shirt) and his wife, Margaret (the lady in the black dress with the white necklace), can be seen greeting customers. The patrons obviously dressed up for their shopping experience. The name "Sendik" was acquired through a simple misunderstanding. While attempting to purchase a stove, "Great Grandpa" Balistreri asked the sales clerk to "send it" to him. The salesman mistook it for Mr. Balistreri's last name, and wrote the delivery order to "Mr. Sendik."

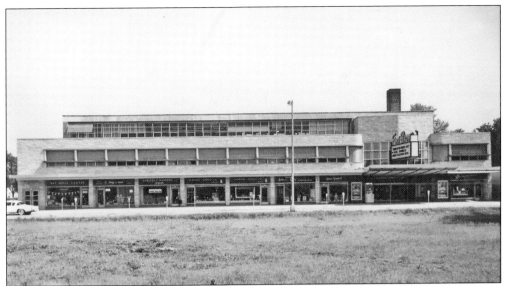

The Man in the White Suit, featuring Alec Guinness, was showing when this 1951 picture of the Fox Bay Building was taken. The business tenants of the building at that time can be seen as, from left to right, the Bay Music Center, C. Benz and Sons (hobby supplies), Chester F. Hartung (carpeting), Schwanke-Kasten Jewelers, John E. ? Photographer, Louise Goodell (women's clothing), and Heinemann's Restaurant. The field across from the building was vacant at the time.

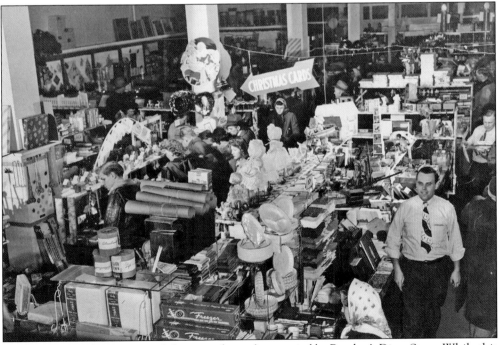

Winkie's Variety Store acquired the space formerly occupied by Raydon's Dime Store. While this December 1947 photograph was taken at another Winkie's store, it illustrates what the original Winkie's store looked like. In this view, Wilbur Winkie (yes, there was a Mr. Winkie) can be seen in the far right side of the photograph in a white shirt. Don Stulmacher is pictured in the lower right corner.

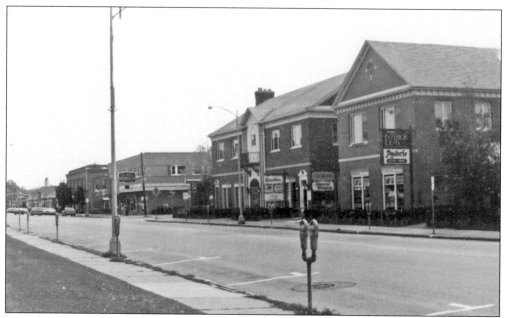

The 100 East block of Silver Spring Drive hasn't changed much from this 1983 street view, although many of the tenants have changed hands. At the time of this photograph, tenants of the buildings included (from left) Heritage Bank, General Electronics, Les Moise, Workbench, Circa Unlimited, Parties Perfect, Roob Photography, TLC Toys, Guenther Flowers and Interiors, I See London, Interior Ideas, Material Things, and Panache.

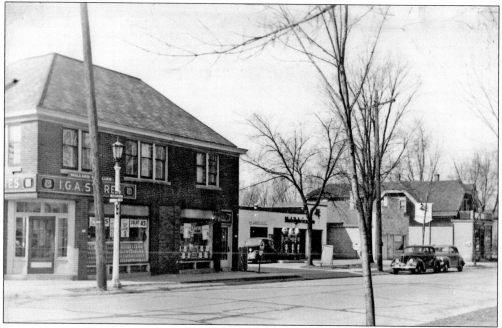

Henry Clay was once a major shopping district in Whitefish Bay. This 1965 view shows the south side of the street between Woodruff and Elkhart. Stores included, from left to right, an IGA Food Store, the Bay Cycle Shop, Gerber's Mobile Auto Service, and Nellie Jones's house and grocery store. Incredibly, the village once had 15 food stores—many of the mom and pop variety.

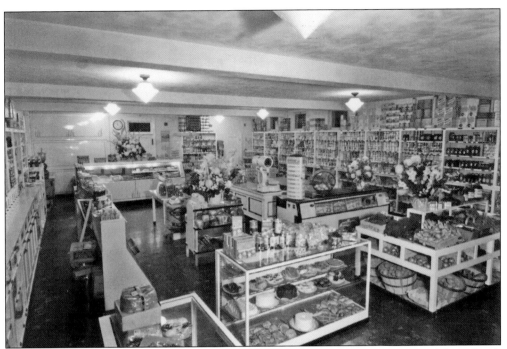

The Henry Pieper food store at 629 East Henry Clay Street was similar to many of the village's other food stores. They were typically stocked with Roundy, Richelieu, Sun-Kist, and Libby brand names in cans, Luick milk and ice cream, and penny candy. At family-oriented places such as this, you got to know your grocer well. (Courtesy of the Milwaukee County Historical Society)

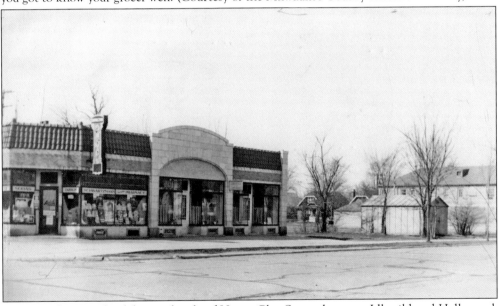

This is a photograph of the south side of Henry Clay Street, between Idlewild and Hollywood. Schwartzman's Pharmacy was on the corner—the rest of the building appears to have been occupied at the time by the First Church of Christ Scientist. The metal building was a *Milwaukee Journal* newspaper station (where paper boys picked up their newspapers). Many of the stores on Henry Clay were torn down in the 1970s for apartment construction.

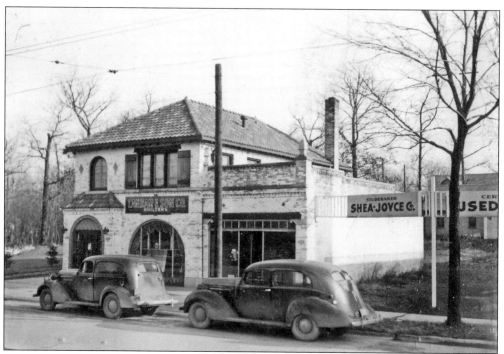

This January 1939 photograph shows an attractive Spanish-influenced commercial building at 4526 North Oakland Avenue. At the time it was occupied by Lanham and Sons. To the south was a car lot known as Cumberland Motor Sales and Cumberland Garage and Service. It was eventually replaced by a Mobile gas station, which was demolished in 2009.

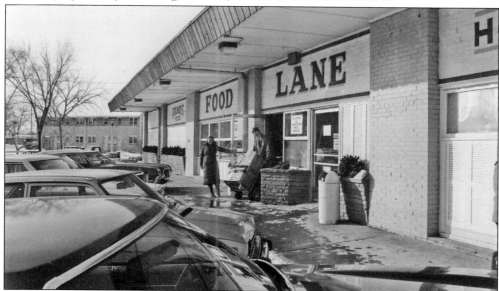

Food Lane located at 240 East Hampton Road was one of the first modern grocery stores in Whitefish Bay with a parking lot offering commuters a convenient way to stop and shop. Owned by the Oleszak family, it was constructed in 1953. It was destroyed in a fire on May 17, 1991. Oleszak opened a new store in September 1993 but was forced to close it in 1995, having lost too many regular customers during the hiatus.

Built in 1914 by George D. Bentley, this restaurant has been a popular Whitefish Bay destination for almost 100 years. Bentley sold the enterprise to John and Anna Pandl in 1915. The Pandl family has operated the restaurant ever since. In this picture, Jack Pandl is pictured with his sister Helen, under a sign that advertized their continuing motto— "You are a stranger here but once."

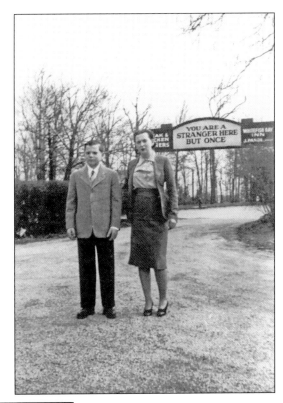

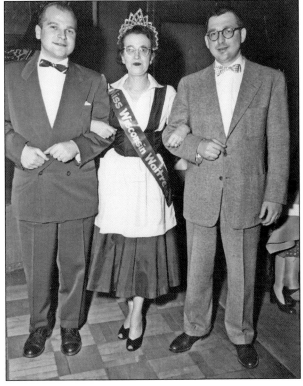

Brothers Jack, left, and George Pandl are pictured with the Miss Wisconsin Waitress of the Year. Jack Pandl owned and ran Pandl's Whitefish Bay Inn at Lake Drive and Woodburn Street. His brother George owned and operated a restaurant farther north along Lake Drive in Bayside.

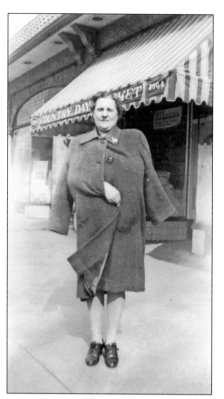

Violet Dumke stands in front of Country Day Market on North Santa Monica Boulevard and Montclaire. The building formerly housed Borgeson Grocery and Diers Meats. After Country Day Market closed, the building became home to Bear Pharmacy.

This picture of the 100 West block of Silver Spring Drive was taken in the late 1950s. The brick building to the left in the photograph was constructed as a church and school for Our Savior Lutheran congregation. It was built in 1930 and served in that capacity until 1939. It was then rented as an office building and eventually torn down to accommodate parking for the adjacent Schmidt and Bartelt Funeral Home.

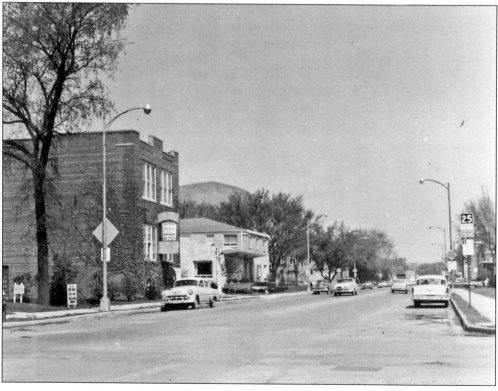

Seven

SOCIAL INFRASTRUCTURE

Education and religion were of primary importance to the early settlers of Whitefish Bay. As residents moved into the area they quickly established schools, churches and voluntary organizations. They also worked to provide recreational opportunities. Joined by Germans and some Irish, these early settlers shaped the community. Their impact can be felt even today.

This chapter begins by highlighting the Whitefish Bay schools, both public and private. Education has always been a priority to village residents. As noted earlier, it was because of the lack of reasonable school access that the community was founded. The community and its residents have worked to create and support a strong school system that has generated great results. At the same time, a number of exemplary private schools have also flourished in the village.

The village's social infrastructure is also represented by the many churches present within the community. Most of these churches are pictured in these pages. In reading the individual church histories, it is amazing how many started services in various village civic buildings until church buildings could be funded and built. As just a few examples, the Pentecostal Lutheran Church held its first services in 1924 at village hall. In 1949, Holy Family Catholic Church held its first masses in the lobby of Whitefish Bay High School. During this time, Bay Shore Lutheran Church was using Cumberland School for worship and Roundy Memorial Baptist Church was using the Whitefish Bay Armory.

This chapter will also attempt to illustrate other aspects of the community's social fabric, including clubs, other organizations and recreational opportunities.

It is not possible to do justice to all of the churches, schools and organizations within the village in a series of 30 or so photographs. This chapter, as a result, only touches the surface—but hopefully helps to capture the heart of the community.

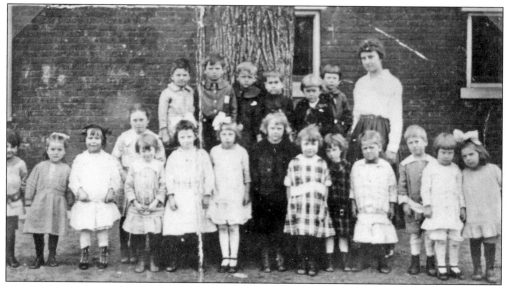

The tradition of the annual school photograph obviously goes back many years. A few of the earliest such photographs from the Whitefish Bay Grade School are reproduced on these pages. This picture was taken outside of the Fleetwood School in about 1915. Carl Geilfuss, who contributed this photograph, is the tall boy in front of the tree.

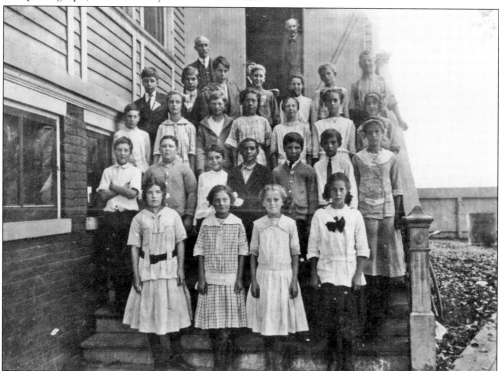

This 1918 photograph likely contains many of the same students from above, now three years older. These students are from grades five through eight. They are photographed on the steps of the school building, with their instructors behind them—all wearing their Sunday best for picture day.

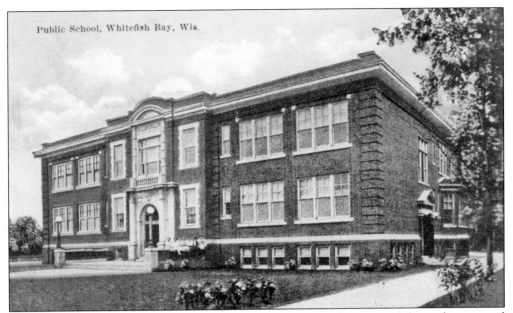

This photograph of Henry Clay School is reproduced from a color postcard dating from around 1930. Henry Clay School is the village's longest-surviving school building; having replaced the original Fleetwood School building after a fire destroyed it. It is now the site of the Whitefish Bay Middle School, a school of approximately 650 students attending grades six, seven, and eight. It was recently named one of the top 100 middle schools in the United States.

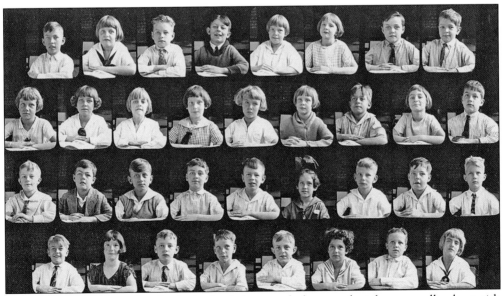

As photography advanced, individual school photographs began to be taken annually, along with a class photograph. This montage from Whitefish Bay Historical Society's photographic collection lines them all up. Presumably such groupings were given to the teacher and the administration. The date these pictures were taken is unknown.

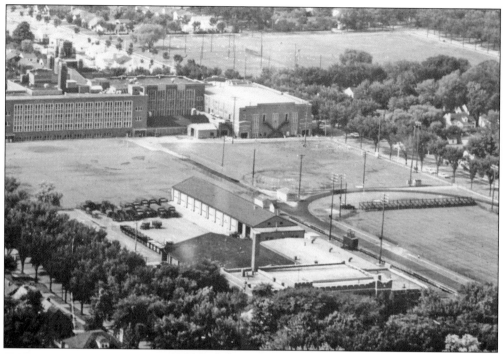

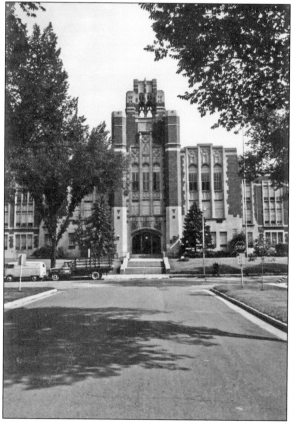

Until 1932, Whitefish Bay did not have a high school. Bay students went to Shorewood High School, Country Day, Downer Seminary, or Milwaukee University School. When Shorewood shut its doors to tuition students, Whitefish Bay finally acted to build its own high school. Until it was completed, high school classes were accommodated at the recently completed Richard's School. This aerial image of the high school appears to be from the 1950s. Page 56 shows an image from 1936.

This 1967 image of Whitefish Bay High School is framed by the trees on Wildwood Avenue. The original building was designed in the Collegiate Gothic style and has been expanded several times, including additions for the Memorial Gymnasium, Laycock Hall (the auditorium), the English Wing, and Memorial Field House. The school newspaper is called the *Tower Times*, named after the tower shown in this photograph.

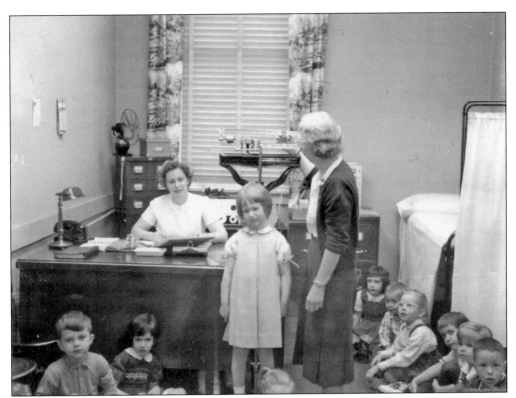

Grade school students are shown visiting the school nurse, in this undated photograph. The nurse is believed to be Margaret Hogenson, who served the school system for many years.

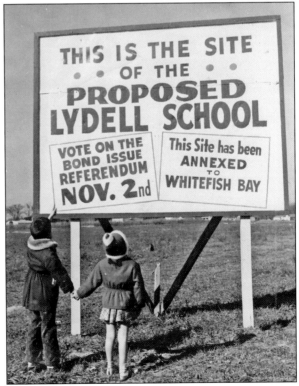

The baby boom following the return of soldiers from World War II affected Whitefish Bay classroom needs. In 1955, the village acquired property from Glendale on Lydell Avenue and annexed it to the village. This photograph shows a sign encouraging residents to vote in favor of a bond referendum authorizing the construction of the Lydell School.

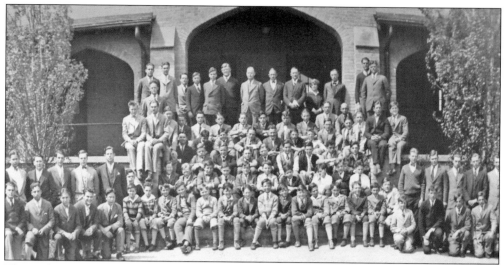

The students and faculty from Milwaukee Country Day School posed in this 1926 picture. The school was founded in 1851 as the German-English Academy. Some Whitefish Bay students went to this school until the village began its own high school program in the 1930s. The school's name eventually changed to University School and in more recent years the buildings and property were sold to the Milwaukee Jewish Federation as the Karl Jewish Community Campus.

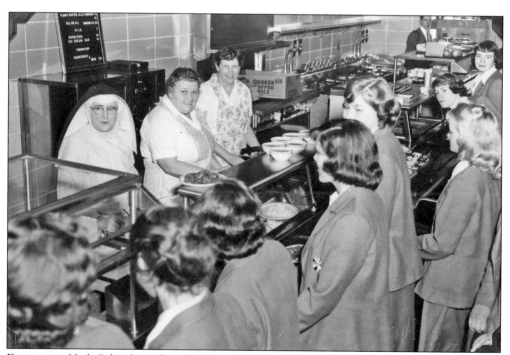

Dominican High School was founded in 1956, fulfilling a longtime dream of Fr. Peter Dietz, the first pastor of St. Monica's congregation. The parish transferred eight acres of land on its west boundary to the Dominican Sisters, who then built the high school. A co-ed college preparatory school, it has graduated nearly 8,000 students. Here Sr. Mary Maxentia is shown overseeing the cafeteria operation in the late 1950s.

The first services of Pentecostal Evangelical Lutheran Church were held in the old Whitefish Bay Village Hall by Pastor Edmund Ebert on June 29, 1924. The white frame building pictured was their original church on the south side of Henry Clay Street. It was replaced by the congregation's current building at 900 East Henry Clay Street. In 1965 the congregation merged with Divine Charity Lutheran Church of Milwaukee. The combined congregation was named Divinity-Divine Charity Lutheran Church.

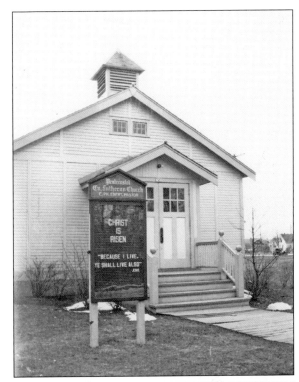

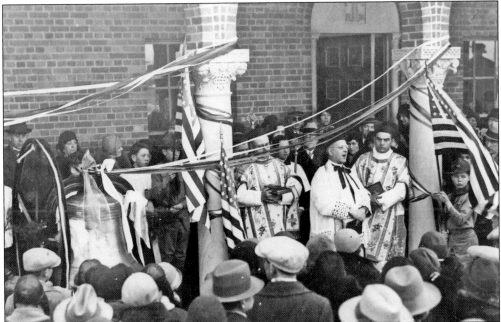

In this Blessing of the Bells service, Fr. Peter Dietz, the first pastor of St. Monica Catholic Parish, can be seen immediately to the left of the right column, In the 1920s, Father Dietz obtained funds to purchase two farms just north of Silver Spring Drive for the parish, partially funded with gifts given to him by several unions in appreciation for his work in the labor movement. The first parish Mass was celebrated at Village Hall on Christmas Day, 1923.

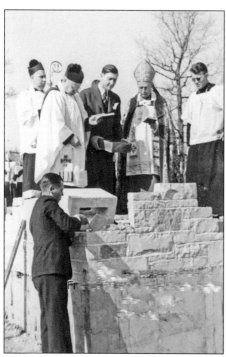

The first church building for Christ Church Episcopal Church, known as the "Little White Church," was built on the south side of Beaumont Avenue in 1931. The current church, on the northwest corner of Beaumont Avenue and Lake Drive, was constructed in 1941. This photograph shows the laying of the cornerstone. Pictured, from left to right, are Fr. Lightfood, Fr. Day, Milton Borman, Bishop Ivins, and Sheldon Beyer. The stonemason could not be identified.

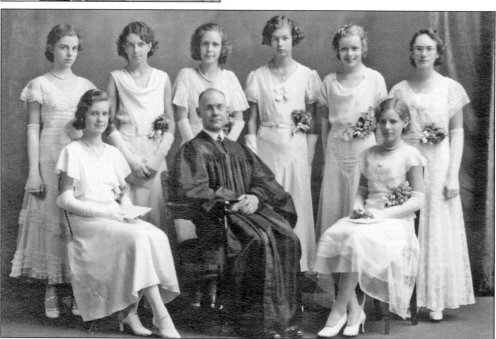

Rev. Paul Bishop of Bay Shore Lutheran Church is shown with the 1932 confirmation class. The congregation was founded in 1929 and the first church building was on the south side of Hampton Road, just west of Marlborough Drive (then called Humboldt Avenue). Rev. Bishop was pastor from 1931 to 1949, when he was called to assume duties as president of the Northwest Synod. His promotion occurred just as the present brick church at 1200 East Hampton Road was nearing completion.

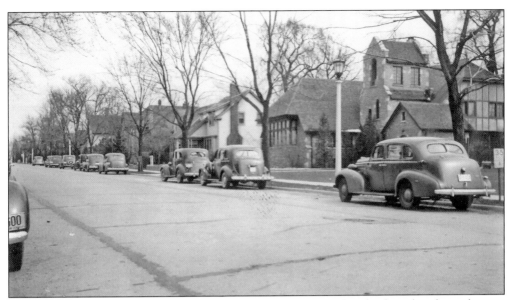

This 1938 photograph shows the Community Methodist Church. The first church on this site dates back to June 1895 when Bishop Isaac Nicholson of the Episcopalian Church acquired the site and built St. Clements, a white frame church with a steeple. A fire from an overheated furnace in 1921 destroyed the building and in 1924, this church was constructed. In 1942 the congregation voted overwhelmingly to affiliate with the Methodist Church.

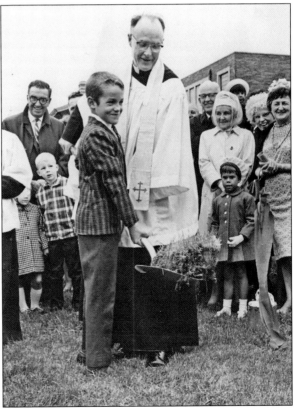

When Holy Family Catholic Church was founded in 1949, "10.5 acres of weeds and swamp" were purchased on Hampton Road. Until a building could be constructed, Sunday masses were held in the lobby of Whitefish Bay High School. St. Monica's Chapel, which had been converted from a barn, was used for smaller services. Here first pastor, Fr. George Wollet, is shown in a groundbreaking ceremony for the new church—the school having been constructed first.

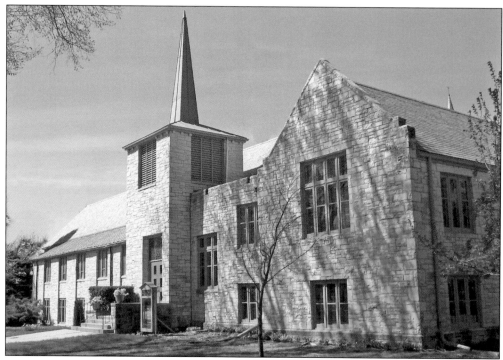

Calling itself the Ardmore Avenue Baptist Chapel, this Baptist congregation held its first service in the Whitefish Bay armory in September 1933. In 1936 the congregation was incorporated and adopted the name Roundy Memorial Baptist Church in honor of J. A. Roundy, a devout pioneer Baptist and cofounder of the firm that became Roundy's Wholesale Foods. J. A. Roundy donated funds that served as the financial base for the church.

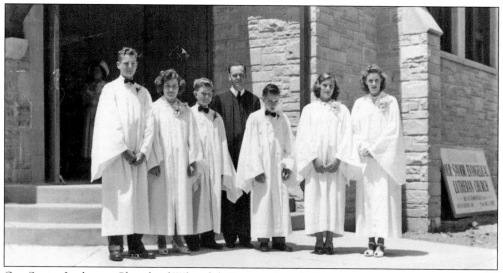

Our Savior Lutheran Church of Whitefish Bay was founded as a mission church in 1930 and a combination chapel and school building was erected at 116 West Silver Spring Drive. A more modern church structure was built to address the continued growth of the congregation at 6021 North Santa Monica Boulevard. This 1949 photograph is of the first confirmation class in the new church with Reverend Harold Schwertfeger.

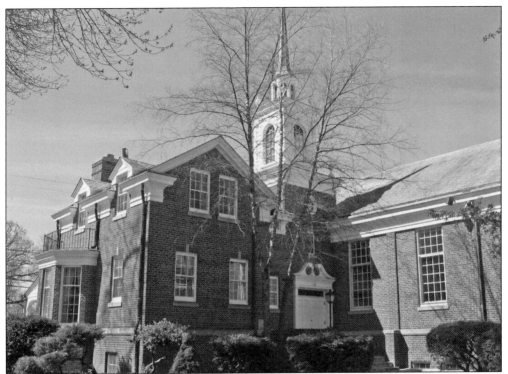

The First Church of Christ Scientist of Whitefish Bay was founded in 1943 and had its initial headquarters at 627 East Henry Clay Street (see the bottom photograph on page 83). Services were held there and Sunday school was held in the auditorium of Henry Clay School. The new building on East Silver Spring Drive, shown here, was dedicated in 1951.

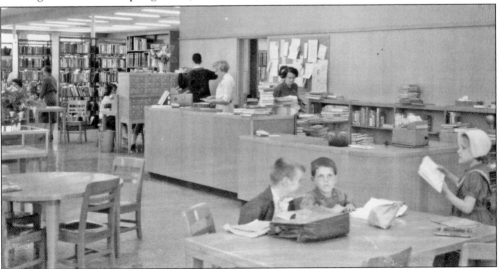

The original Whitefish Bay library was located in the basement of the old village hall, located at the intersection of Marlborough Drive and Lexington Boulevard. In addition to the library, there was also a bookmobile that covered the village. This image is from the interior of the library, constructed in 1955. The building was almost entirely replaced with a new structure at the same location in 2002.

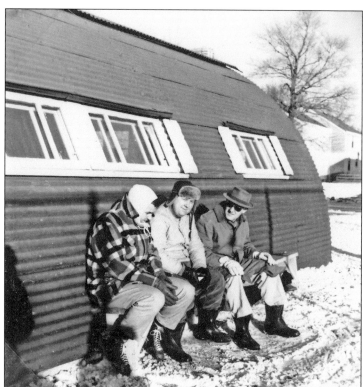

Cahill Park, also referred to as Cahill Square, was developed in the 1950s. Prior to that, the area was called the "Y" because of the configuration of railroad tracks that coursed the area. A Quonset hut once stood at the approximate location of the current recreation building. It appears that the young man on the left is wearing ice skates. His identity, as well as that of the other men, could not be determined.

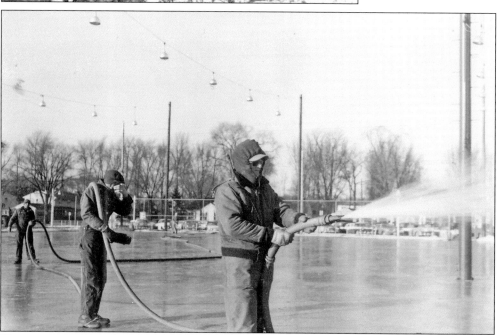

These men appear to be workers from the village's department of public works. They are shown flooding the ice rink at Cahill Park. The tennis courts apparently were used as the location of the ice rink in the 1950s. Earlier records indicate that the high school football field was once flooded in the winter for ice skating.

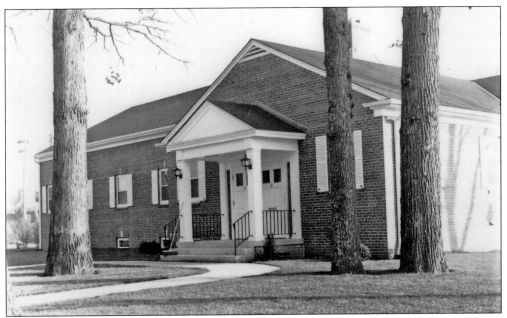

The Silver Spring Masonic Lodge was charted in 1926 and met in the Whitefish Bay Community Church (now called United Methodist Church of Whitefish Bay) until 1942. The lodge then moved to the Christ Church Episcopal Mission Building at 517 East Beaumont Avenue. The lodge eventually purchased the old mission building and site from Christ Church in about 1960 and erected the current Federal-style building in 1964.

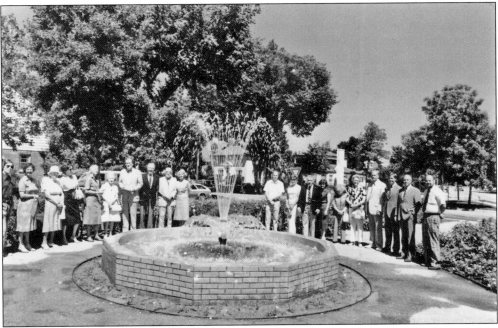

This photograph is of the dedication of the fountain in School House Park. The fountain was a gift of Dorothy (Orton) Inbush, who is shown standing at the immediate left of center, along with the members of the Whitefish Bay Civic Improvement Association. School House Park is the site of the first Whitefish Bay School Building.

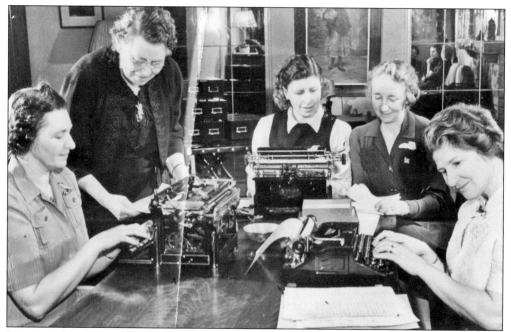

Members of the Whitefish Bay Women's Club are shown at work on the 1941 village phone directory in the basement of Florence Knoernschild's home. Shown are Lydia Martini, Amanda Schleif, Mary Tobin, Irene Travism and Blanche Fieldler. The first Whitefish Bay Directory was published by the Club in 1927. In 1941, they began publishing a combined Whitefish Bay–Fox Point Directory.

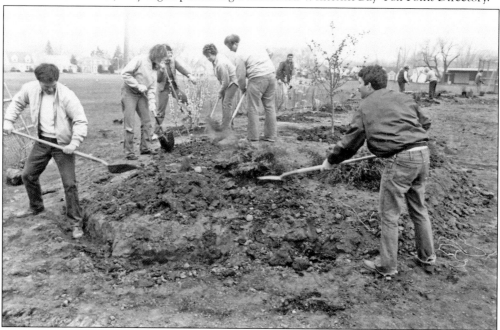

Village residents have a long tradition of service to the community. Here volunteers are pictured working on the landscaping for a new playground at Cahill Square in 1983. The Cahill Park recreation building and warming house can be seen in the background at the upper right of the photograph. This picture was taken before the pitched roof was added.

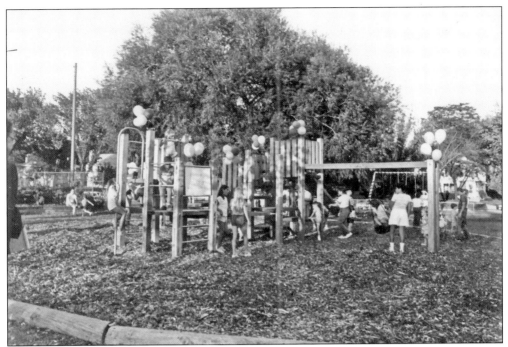

Volunteerism provides many benefits to the community, as evidenced by the happy children using the new playground equipment at Cahill Square in this August 1984 photograph.

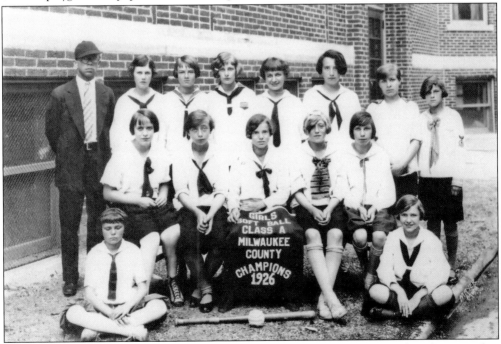

Whitefish Bay school athletic teams have been so successful over the years that championship photographs could fill this book. This picture is of the 1926 girls Milwaukee County Class A softball champions from Henry Clay School with their coach, Chet Wangerin, is offered as a single representative example.

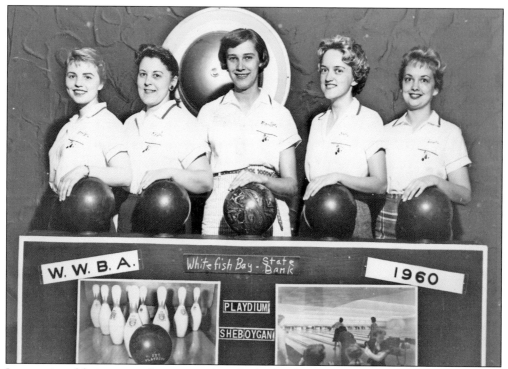

Interest in athletic events does not end at the high school level. Many Whitefish Bay adults continue to participate in various sporting activities and leagues. Some leagues, of course, are sponsored by companies, as in this photograph of the Whitefish Bay State Bank at the Wisconsin Women's Bowling Association state tournament in 1960. Judging from the smiles on their faces, they must have had a successful tournament.

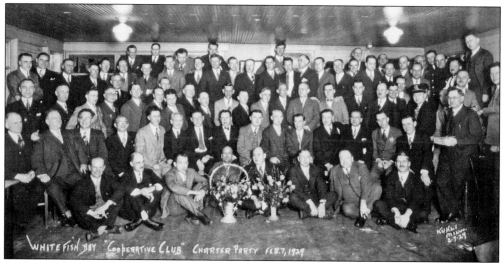

As the caption states, this was the charter party of the Whitefish Bay "Co-operative Club," held on February 7, 1929. It appears that the club supported Whitefish Bay school athletic activities, judging from various newspaper articles. A former resident recalls that the club had its meetings at Shorewood High School at the time. The gentleman on the right is holding a cigar box—presumably to distribute to the group after the photograph.

Eight
THE CHANGING LANDSCAPE

The changes to Whitefish Bay have often been subtle: a building goes up here, another is moved or razed, an owner adds an addition, a road is resurfaced, a restaurant opens, a grocery store closes. With the passage of many years, the accumulation of such changes results in a dramatic transformation.

This section attempts to illustrate some of the changes that have occurred to the community through the years, as well as some proposed changes that never materialized. These pictures include a number of old street scenes—images that may help show the contrasts between then and now. Some of these pictures of early roads reveal how sparsely the community was occupied in the 1920 and early 1930s.

In a September 1931 interview by the *Whitefish Bay Herald*, Thomas E. Callahan, former resident and village official, reminisced about the changes that had occurred in the village since 1910. He noted that the village once had, "rough, dirty roads with plank sidewalks half rotted away. There were no lights on the streets and only one store, which also contained the post-office." Callahan reported that he was dumbfounded at the growth of the village during his absence. Perhaps many of the readers of this book will also be astonished by some of these early images of the village.

This entire book, of course, can be viewed as an illustration of the changes that have occurred in Whitefish Bay—changes that will continue to occur. Hopefully it will also help to connect us to the past.

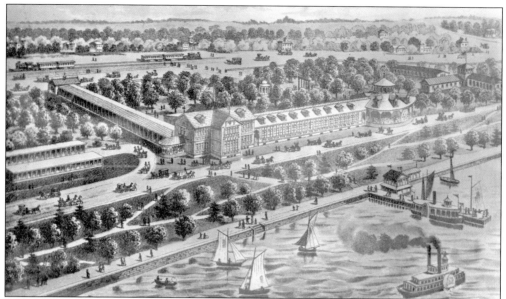

This chapter starts with an illustration of a proposal that never occurred. Developers had once planned a massive hotel and resort project, to be built where Palisades Road is currently located. From the images of trains, horse drawn carriages and steam boats, it is evident that this project was targeted for the late 1800s. Whether it may have been a competing proposal to the Pabst Whitefish Bay Resort is unknown.

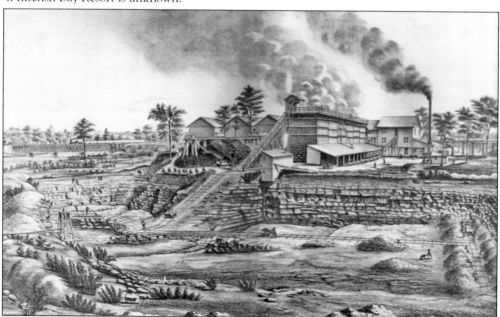

In 1873, Joseph Berthelet discovered mineral deposits adjacent to the Milwaukee River suitable for making cement. He acquired the land, perfected the techniques and ran a large successful operation beginning in 1876. Subsequent technological changes in the cement industry forced the company to close the operation in 1911. In 1916, Milwaukee County bought the company's land on the east side of the river and established Estabrook Park, the first unit in the county's system of parks.

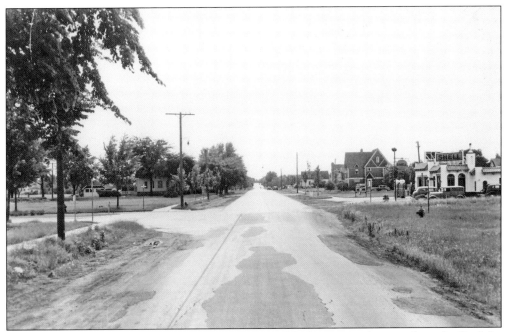

This is Hampton Road and Santa Monica Boulevard looking east. Amazingly with all of the changes that have occurred at this intersection since the 1930s, a Shell Oil Filing Station continues to stand on this same corner. The home on the left is a farmhouse built by Ludwig Leu for his family. It was later occupied by Adelaide Mohr.

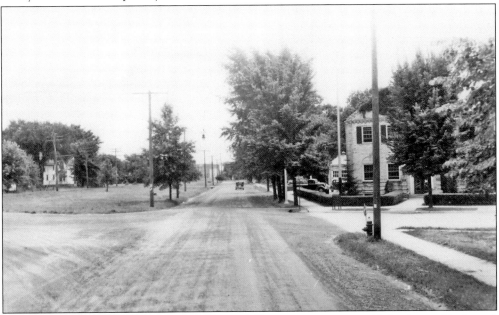

This view is looking southeast down Marlborough Drive as it intercepts with Lexington Boulevard. The brick building to the right is the second Whitefish Bay Village Hall. The wide expanse to the west of the intersection is the right-of-way for the Chicago and Northwestern Railway, even though only the streetcar ran through this area at the time. If you look up the street you may observe that it ends several blocks north. Marlborough did not yet extend to Silver Spring Drive.

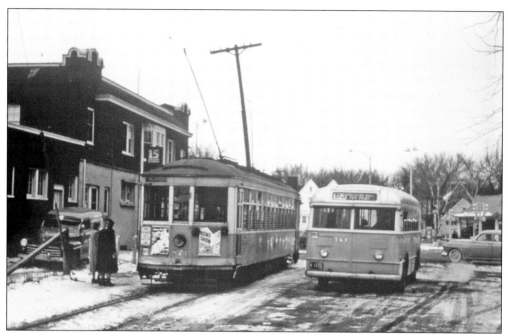

This photograph is a good illustration of change. The No. 15 streetcar is being passed by a new city bus in this 1946 picture. This view is looking north toward the intersection of Marlborough and Silver Spring. The building on the left housed the Whitefish Bay Pharmacy and an IGA grocery store (see page 73).

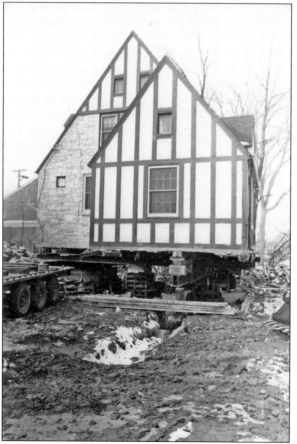

In viewing village records, an amazing number of homes have been relocated during the years. Often this occurred as houses were adjusted to accommodate the layout of streets once the village was subdivided. Others, such as this relocation of the former Christ Church parsonage, were necessitated by development plans—in this case to provide additional parking for Sendik's. The house was moved to the 4700 block of Oakland Avenue.

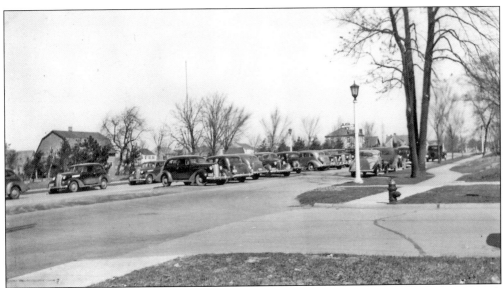

Cars are parked on the Santa Monica Boulevard median during Sunday Mass at St. Monica's congregation in 1938. This view looks northwest from East Beaumont Avenue. The barn in the background belonged to the Timpel/Fleming farm. This had been their farmland prior to its purchase by the congregation.

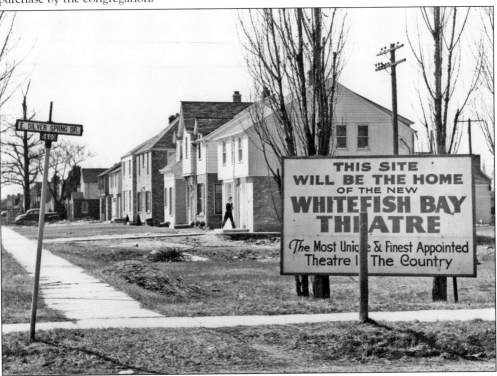

Two theaters were once planned for Whitefish Bay. One we all know now as the Fox Bay Cinema Theatre. The other was planned by Marcus Corporation in 1947 for the corner of Silver Spring and Kent. Presumably, it was cancelled once the competing theater was built a couple of blocks away.

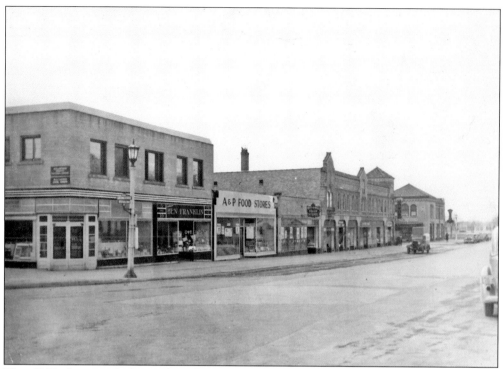

This 1939 photograph shows the Silver Spring shopping district, looking southwest. While the buildings displayed in the picture continue to grace the street, all of the stores have changed hands.

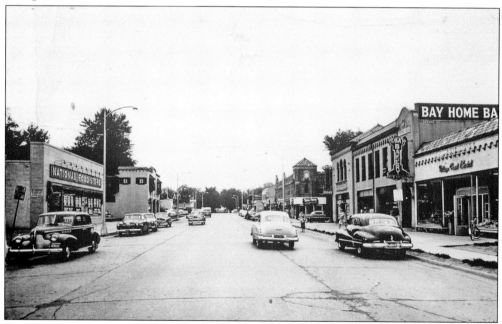

By the time this picture was taken, the downtown shopping center was looking much more vibrant. This image, looking east along Silver Spring Drive, must have been taken in the early 1950s, judging from the vehicles.

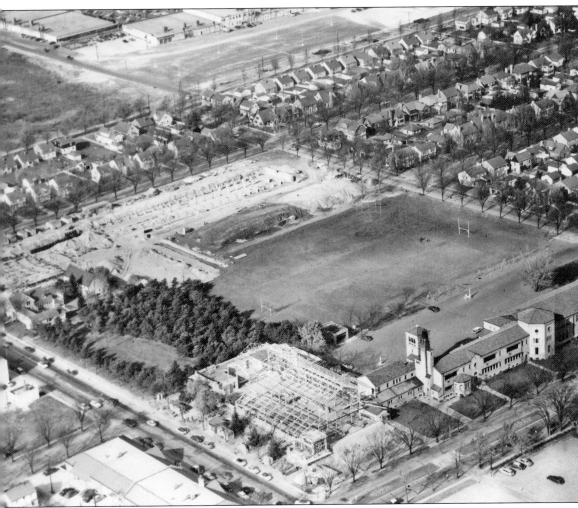

In this November 1954 aerial photograph, construction is underway on the church for St. Monica's congregation and the school building for Dominican High School. Some of the land was purchased in 1923 from Bernard Geilfuss, who originally farmed the area. On the left of the photograph, Bernard Geilfuss's house and barn can be seen. These structures were converted by St. Monica's parish into a rectory and chapel. The barn-chapel served the early parish, until new buildings could be constructed. At the top of this picture, portions of the initial buildings for the Bayshore Shopping Center can be observed. The shopping center was built in 1953—at the time there were only a few such shopping centers in the United States.

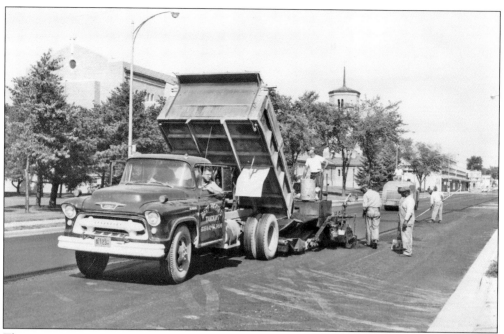

The major streetscaping project on Silver Spring Drive in 2008–2009 wasn't the first time that the street was rebuilt. This picture from the 1960s shows asphalt being laid during one of the previous improvement projects on Silver Spring Drive. The street was also reconstructed in 1988.

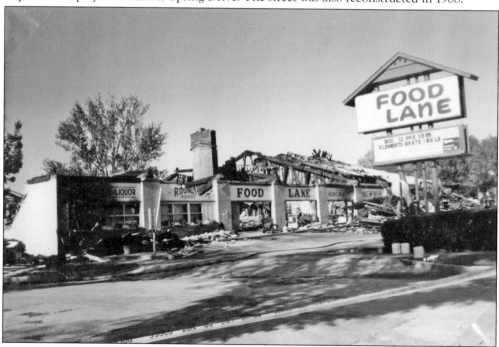

Not all changes were the result of design, as illustrated by this picture of the aftermath of a 1991 fire that destroyed the Food Lane grocery store at Hampton and Santa Monica. While the store was eventually rebuilt, the new Food Lane was unable to recapture its former customer base and closed for financial reasons a few months later.

Nine
The People of the Village

The previous chapters attempted to tell the story of our community from various viewpoints. While many of the pictures in the previous chapters show buildings and objects, this chapter illustrates the lives of the people that have lived here and who have established the community. Shown here are images of the people of Whitefish Bay—people with their families, soldiers returning from war, people going to the doctor, kids at play—essentially people just going about their lives in the community.

Since the village's formation in 1892 with 312 individuals living within its boundaries, the community has grown to approximately 14,000 people. While a tally of the total number of people that have lived or worked in the village has never been attempted, it is evident that the number is in the hundreds of thousands.

The illustrations in this chapter only cover a few dozen residents among these thousands. The pictures are offered as a representative sample of the many people that lived in the village during its first 100 years.

Whitefish Bay surveyed residents a few years ago to inquire why they chose to live in the community. Residents responded that they chose to live in Whitefish Bay because the village offers a sense of community, high-quality public and private schools, well-maintained private and public property, diverse and well maintained houses, and a safe environment. It appears that present day residents of Whitefish Bay share many of the same reasons for choosing to live here as past inhabitants.

Although Whitefish Bay is considered a part of the Greater Milwaukee area, the village still retains the feeling of a much smaller community. Residents get to know one another and see each other in the local stores, as well as at the schools and churches. They also enjoy gathering for various community events such as community concerts, ice cream socials, Fourth of July parade and fireworks, sidewalk sales, the pumpkin display, the Sounds of Summer concert, the Holiday Stroll, and other activities.

Whitefish Bay remains an excellent place to live.

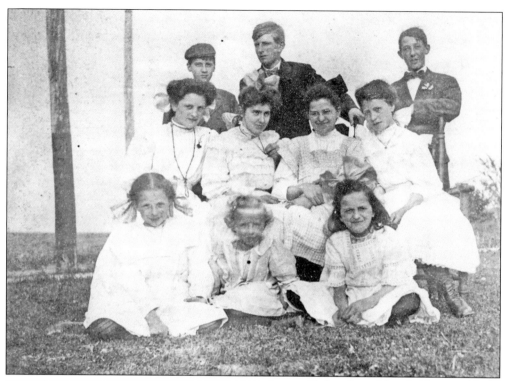

Only a few of the children could be identified in this photograph taken in 1907 or 1908. In the back row, middle, is Alvin Scheife and to his right is Al Knop. The girl in the middle row on the right is Elsie Knop. The Scheifes owned and operated Whitefish Bay's first general store and were among its earliest residents.

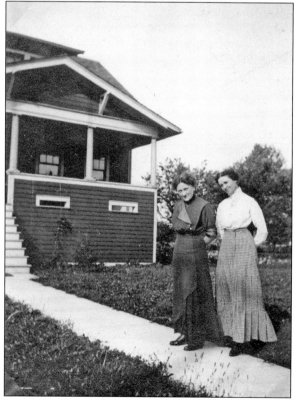

The women standing outside of 400 East Lake View Avenue in this 1911 photograph are Mrs. Thomas (Kreese) Nell and Mrs. Lule (Ford) Byrne. Mrs. Byrne was a teacher at the first Whitefish Bay School. The house was the Callahan home. Tom Callahan was the chief of police and held a number of other village positions.

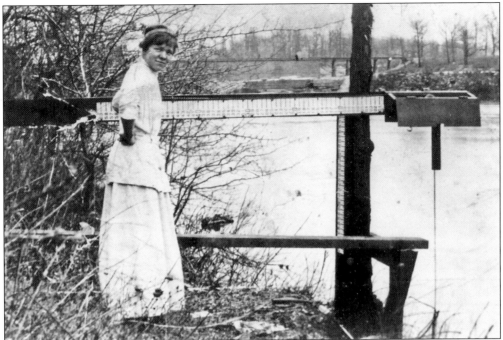

In the early 1900s, the level of the Milwaukee River was monitored regularly. In this photograph, taken about 1916, Johanna Roth is pictured observing the mechanism used to monitor the level of the river water.

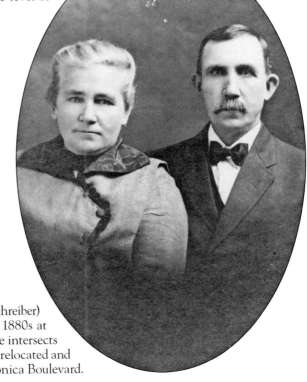

This portrait is of Julius and Pauline (Schreiber) Leu. The Leus built a home in the 1880s at approximately where Idlewild Avenue intersects Hampton Road. The house was later relocated and is presently at 5020 North Santa Monica Boulevard.

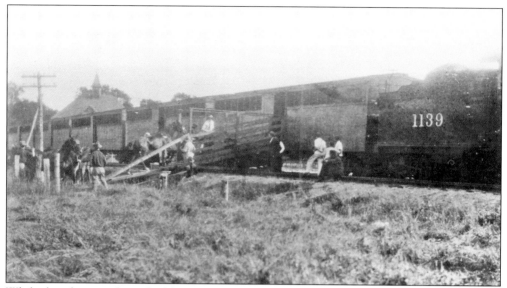

While this photograph is a bit blurry, in it the National Guard can be observed loading cavalry horses on the train for annual training. The building with the steeple, seen behind the freight cars, is the Welcome Park pavilion. It is believed that the photograph was taken between 1915 and 1917. (Courtesy of Peter Haupt.)

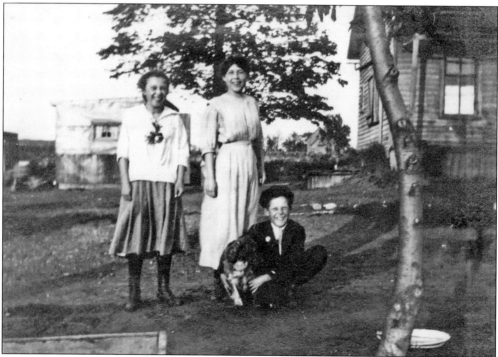

Lydia, Dora and Elmer Runge are pictured on their parent's farm in this 1918 picture. They were the children of Elmer Runge and Annie Mohr. The farmhouse, located between Ardmore and Wildwood just north of Hampton Road was built by the Kruse family and later rented by the Krueger and Runge families. The property is now the site of two churches, Bay Shore Lutheran and Roundy's Memorial Baptist Church.

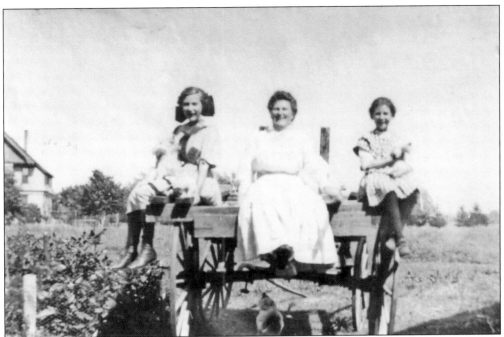

This photo was taken about 1906 in the yard of Joseph Julian. Lillian Scheife, daughter of Lillian Julian and Henry Scheife, is pictured on the left. Her cousin, Ollie Julian is on the right side of the wagon. The woman in the middle is unknown. (Courtesy of Olive Julian Schroeder.)

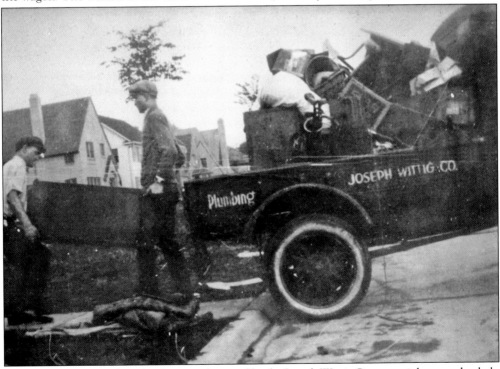

In this 1928 photograph, a plumbing truck owned by the Joseph Wittig Company is borrowed to help move the Haupt family into their new home at 614 East Beaumont. (Courtesy of Peter Haupt.)

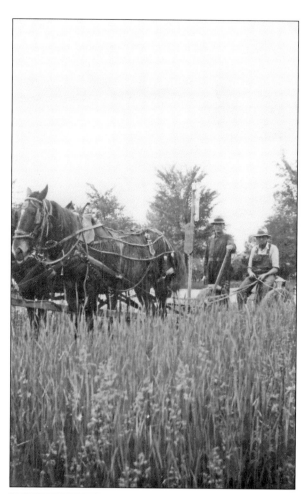

As late as 1937, Whitefish Bay hired a crew that used a team of horses to cut weeds along some of the village's roads. This view taken at Lake Drive and School Road shows Arthur Weise of Whitefish Bay and John Roden of Grafton driving a team of horses owned by Ben Gotthard. The signs say "Bus Stop" and "Fire Zone."

This 1939 photograph was taken in the back yard of 5861 North Kent and shows two mothers playing with their children on what must have been a warm summer day. (Courtesy of Milwaukee County Historical Society.)

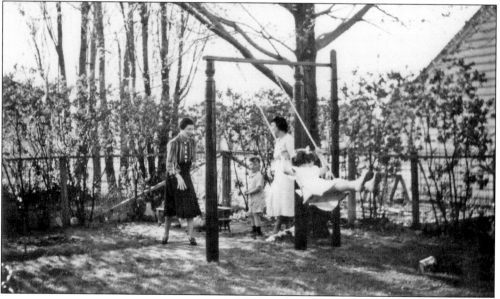

Soldiers are pictured during a ceremony outside of the Whitefish Bay Armory. During the Second World War, solders from the Wisconsin National Guard trained at the armory and eventually formed part of the army's 32nd Division. They were involved in the New Guinea campaign, as well as other activity during World War II. (Courtesy of Peter Haupt.)

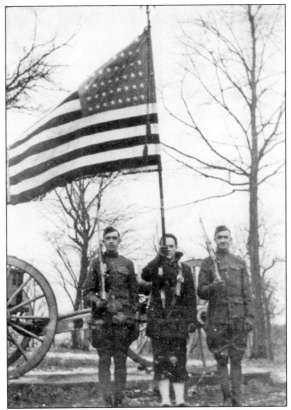

This is another view of soldiers being trained at the Whitefish Bay Armory during the early 1940s. A home on North Ardmore Avenue can be seen in the background.

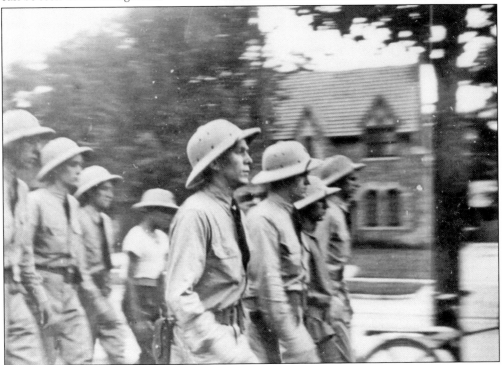

117

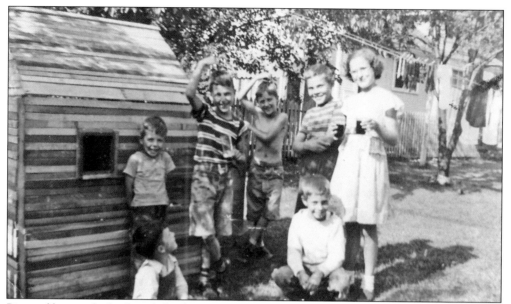

Pictured here is the backyard play house at 5135 North Woodruff. It was covered with lath strips and built next to the family victory garden. The children include Jeff and Art Anderson and Gary, Lynn, and Marlys Ehlenbeck. Village residents planted victory gardens during World War II to reduce the pressure on the public food supply brought on by the war effort. While the war was over by the time this photograph was taken, many families continued to cultivate their gardens.

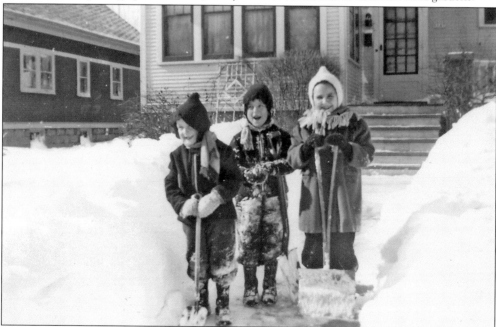

In January 1947, the Milwaukee area was hit with arguably the worst snowstorm to ever hit Milwaukee. In a storm lasting three days, high winds caused huge drifts, some as high as 15 feet. This brought all traffic to a standstill and closed businesses and schools for days. Shortly after the storm passed, Lynn, Gary and Marlys Ehlenbeck are seen shoveling out and enjoying the day off at 5147 North Woodruff.

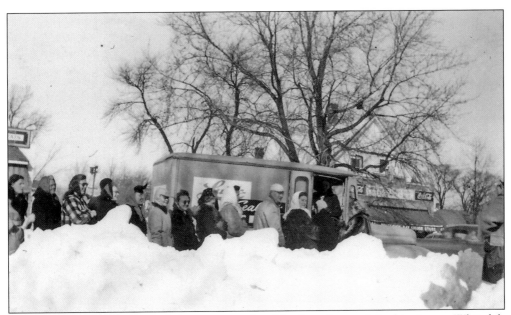

After the blizzard of 1947 subsided, stores were closed for days afterward. In this picture, Whitefish Bay residents are lined up to purchase milk from a Luick delivery truck. Because of the high demand and limited supply, customers could only purchase one bottle per person. This view is of Silver Spring Drive. Shallert's Liquor Store is seen in the background.

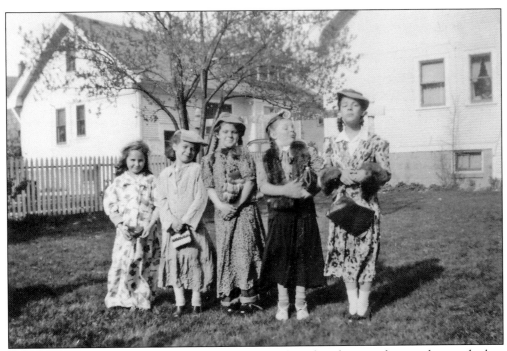

It was obviously dress-up play day in Whitefish Bay when this photograph was taken in the late 1940s. The children include Marlys Ehlenbeck, Barbara Washak (her father, Leo, owned the Bay Cycle Shop), and Mary Ann Aiken (whose father owned the City Service Station).

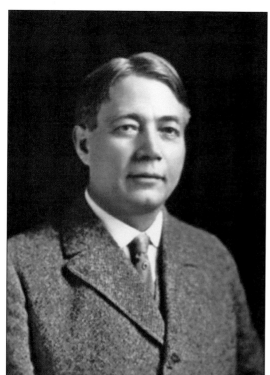

Frank Klode was president of Whitefish Bay between 1914–1918 and 1924–1934. Current residents will recognize his name because of the lakefront park named after him. When the parkland was first purchased, Klode stepped down from his office for an hour to allow the village board to consider the matter. He had a conflict of interest, since he owned the old Grams farm property that became Klode Park.

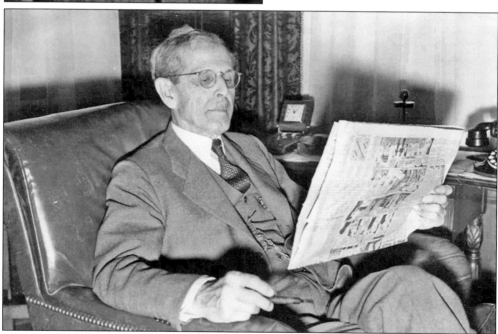

This is William A. Klatte relaxing at home with the daily newspaper. A decade after graduating from the UW Madison Law School's 1899 class, Klatte helped create the position of Milwaukee County clerk of civil court. He served in that position for 30 years. Klatte and his wife, Florence, bought a house at 716 East Day Avenue in 1912. After his death in 1944, Florence continued living there until 1951.

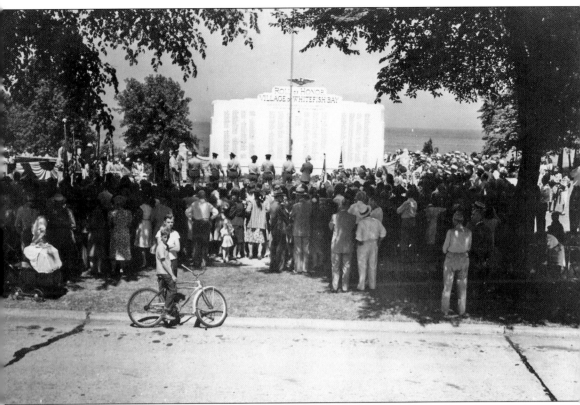

Following World War II, a memorial dedicated to the men and women from the village that served in the armed forces during the war was established on the bluff overlooking Lake Michigan in Buckley Park. This photograph was taken of the dedication ceremony. The wooden memorial deteriorated over time and had to be removed. The eagle from the memorial now resides over the podium in the Whitefish Bay boardroom. In 2010, a new veterans' memorial was dedicated, constructed on the site of the former Whitefish Bay armory. The new memorial pays tribute to veterans of all wars, honors their service and provides a place for remembrance and reflection. The site also serves as a memorial to the 32nd Red Arrow division and Wisconsin's Iron Brigade.

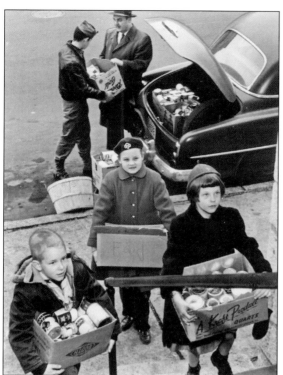

Three scouts from Whitefish Bay (a Cub Scout, Girl Scout, and Brownie Scout) are shown bringing boxes of food to the St. Vincent de Paul Society to be distributed to Hungarian refugees in this December 1956 photograph from the *Milwaukee Journal*. (Courtesy of the Wisconsin Historical Society.)

This photograph from the late 1950s shows a doctor from the Whitefish Bay Health Department administering the new polio vaccine to Polly Packenham. In the early 1950s, the country experienced an outbreak of polio cases. This crippling disease affected as many as 60,000 annually. The first effective polio vaccine was developed in 1952 by Jonas Salk. Soon after his vaccine was licensed in 1955, vaccination campaigns were launched.

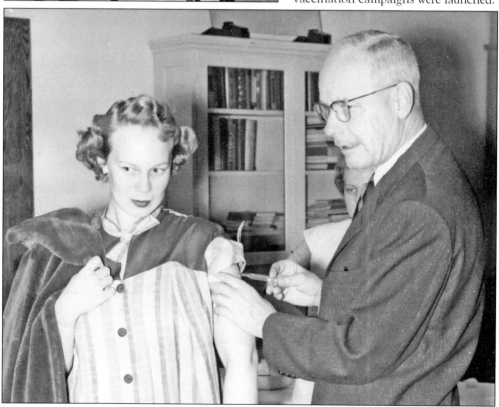

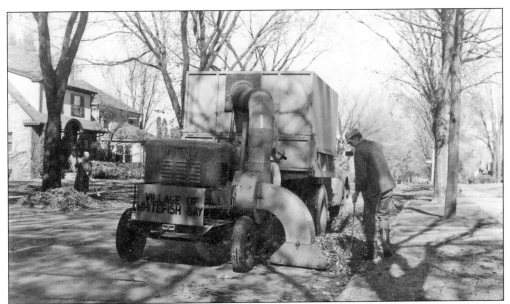

Leaf collection is underway in this fall 1957 photograph. Many of the streets in Whitefish Bay were lined with elm trees, which provided a majestic canopy that arched over the streets. In the 1960s and 1970s Dutch elm disease, which was spread by the elm bark beetle, devastated most of the tree population. The village has since established a much more diverse population of trees.

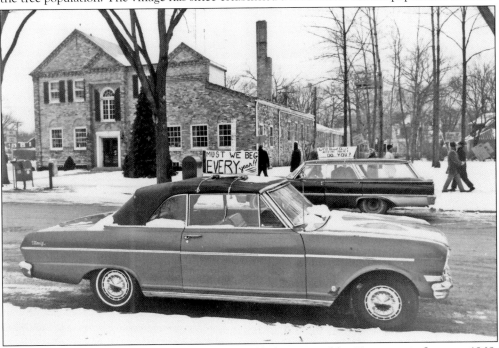

Staff relations in this community have generally been amiable. However, in January 1968, negotiations with the union representing the Whitefish Bay police broke down for a time. In this image, a picket line has been formed outside of village hall. This photograph also provides an interesting perspective of the village's community buildings at Lexington Boulevard and Marlborough Drive.

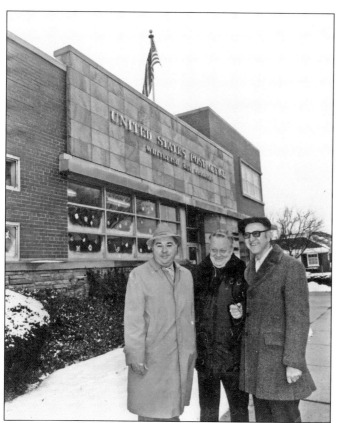

In this photograph taken January 2, 1975, three recent retirees of the U.S. Postal Service pose in front of the former Whitefish Bay branch office, located at 109 East Silver Spring Drive. The building has subsequently been used for retail stores, including the current tenant, Elements East Furnishings.

Municipal employees once plowed sidewalks in Whitefish Bay whenever the snowfall exceeded four inches. In this 1958 photograph the village's Jeep paused its run in order to talk to a resident. The sidewalk plowing service was discontinued in the late 1970s as residents complained about lawn damage and the price of powered snow blowers became more affordable.

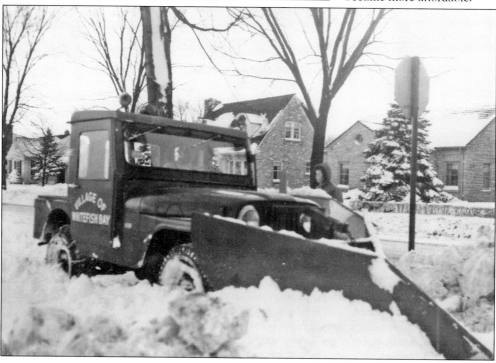

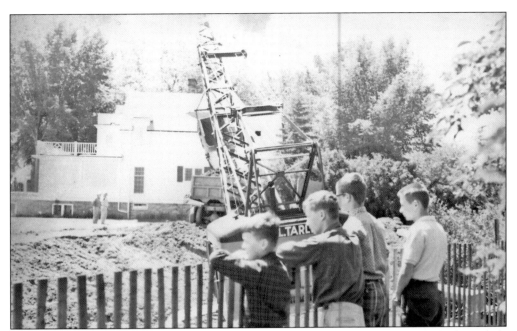

Four Whitefish Bay boys observe construction activities on the new pump house being built at Klode Park in 1961. The facility pumps Lake Michigan water to the Northshore Water Filtration Plant that currently provides potable water to residents of Whitefish Bay, Fox Point, and Glendale.

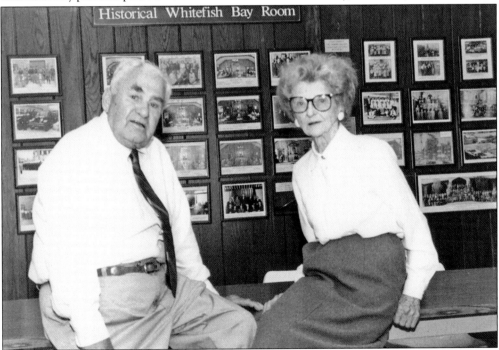

Ralph Knoernschild and Teresa Maegli of the Whitefish Bay Historical Society pose in the historical room at village hall in this photograph from about 1995. The room's walls are filled with framed historical photographs of the village. Knoernschild was a former trustee of the village and served in many other capacities, including president of the historical society.

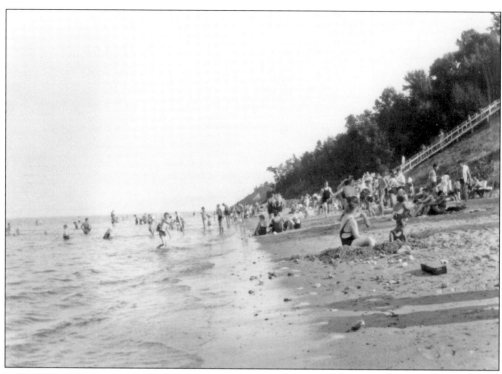

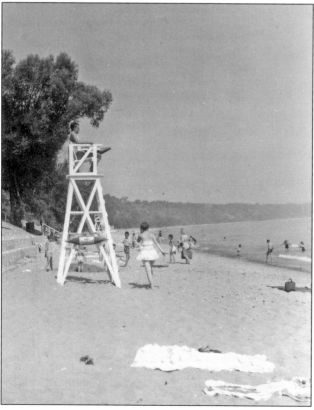

The two photographs on this page illustrate the natural attraction of the beach on the shore of Whitefish Bay during the warm summer months. The top image is believed to be of Klode Park in the 1940s. Notice the lengthy wooden walkway leading down the bluff. The image at left is of Klode Park in 1958. The village once hired and trained student lifeguards during the summer months for the beaches at both Klode and Buckley parks. As late as 1936, the police chief issued a warning in the *Whitefish Bay Herald* that anyone wearing a two-piece swimsuit would be sent home to change. (Top photograph courtesy of the Milwaukee County Historical Society)

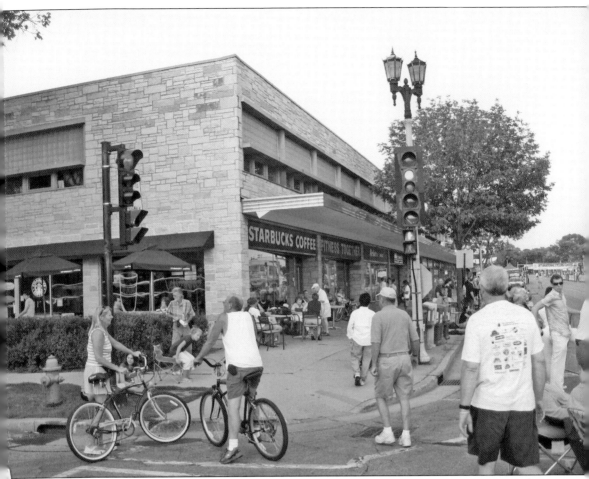

As this more recent photograph illustrates, Whitefish Bay continues to be a vibrant community with many social activities. This picture was taken at the 2008 International Cycling Classic, during the Super Week pro tour. The picture looks northeast at the intersection of Santa Monica Boulevard and Silver Spring Drive and shows the corner of the Fox Bay Building. The Whitefish Bay Civic Foundation sponsors several events annually. Additionally, the Village Business Improvement District holds a number of events each year featuring the Silver Spring business district.

Discover Thousands of Local History Books Featuring Millions of Vintage Images

Arcadia Publishing, the leading local history publisher in the United States, is committed to making history accessible and meaningful through publishing books that celebrate and preserve the heritage of America's people and places.

Find more books like this at
www.arcadiapublishing.com

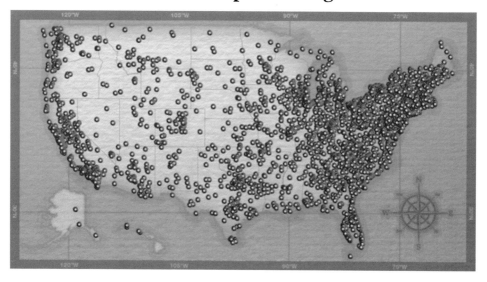

Search for your hometown history, your old stomping grounds, and even your favorite sports team.

Consistent with our mission to preserve history on a local level, this book was printed in South Carolina on American-made paper and manufactured entirely in the United States. Products carrying the accredited Forest Stewardship Council (FSC) label are printed on 100 percent FSC-certified paper.

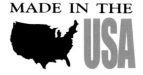